# Online Bookselling

## A Practical Guide With Detailed Explanations And Insightful Tips

by Michael E. Mould

Published by Aardvark Publishing Company, L.L.C.
Email: mike@online-bookselling.com

Michael E. Mould

# Online Bookselling:
## A Practical Guide with Detailed Explanations and Insightful Tips

ISBN: 1599714876 (CD-ROM)
ISBN: 1427600708 (paperback)

First Edition, February 2006, [CD-ROM]
Updated and Expanded Edition, May 2006 (paperback)


10 9 8 7 6 5 4 3 2

Printed in the United States of America

To all those pursuing the path of online bookselling I wish success

# Warning And Disclaimer

The author and publisher shall have neither liability nor responsibility to any person or entity with respect to any loss or damage caused, or alleged to be caused, directly or indirectly by the information contained in this book or the accompanying software. The information, methods, and techniques described by the author are based on his own experience.

They may not work for you and no recommendation is made to follow the same course of action. No representation is made that following the advice in this book or the accompanying software will work in your case. The author and publisher expressly disclaim any and all warranties, including but not limited to warranty of fitness for particular use.

Everyone's financial situation is different. This book and the accompanying software were designed to provide information in regard to the subject matter covered and it is sold with the understanding that the author and publisher are not engaged in rendering legal, accounting, financial planning, or other professional services.

If you feel that legal or other expert assistance is required, the services of a competent professional should be sought. You are urged to read all the material provided in this book and tailor the information to your individual needs.

Every effort has been made to make this book and the accompanying software as complete and accurate as possible. However, there may be mistakes, typographical, mathematical, or in content. Therefore, this book and the accompanying software should be used only as a general guide to assist you with setting up and operating an online bookstore in a manner that suits your specific situation.

# Contents

i x

# Introduction

The industry of used book resale is very rapidly expanding. Only a few years ago, Advanced Book Exchange, Abebooks.com, reported to have only a few hundred used book dealers listing through them, and now the number is in excess of 13,500, listing over 80,000,000 books and selling a total about 20,000 books a day[1]. This should not be discouraging to you; there is still ample room for more booksellers and their books. In fact, Abebooks.com reports that over 4 million unique and new potential customers visit their website looking for books each month.

You should also consider that Abebooks.com is not the only place on the Internet where you can sell used books, nor is it anywhere near the biggest. There are dozens of reputable venues through which you can list and sell your used books to the world, and that is exactly what I intend to teach you throughout this book. Amazon.com is the largest of the online book marketplaces and through Amazon.com about 70% of all online sales occur. That means Amazon.com sells approximately $400,000,000 of books each year! That is almost $46,000 per hour, 24 hours a day, seven days a week.

In this book I will cover all aspects of the on-line used book selling business. I will tell you how to find, sell, price, list, package, and ship your used books. I will also discuss some of the pros and cons of the various listing services and bookseller affiliations that you have access to, and how each may/may not really be to your advantage. I will also tell you how much you should expect to pay for books for your inventory and some long-term planning considerations for your business.

There are all kinds on home-based businesses opportunities available, but very few that offer the return on investment of a home-based bookselling business.

Even if you are already an online bookseller you will find tips here that can save you much more than the cost of buying this book, and the bookkeeping software will help you track and visualize the progress of your business.

I have tried to provide numerous personal experiences to help you relate to what I am describing for you, as well as pictures, graphs, and tables to visually illustrate things where appropriate. There are some out there that hype the online bookselling business with claims of selling more than a million dollars worth of books, or they insinuate that it is easy money. I do not want to make any absurd claims and my success and/or how much money I have made selling books online should be irrelevant to you. It really doesn't matter if I have sold millions of dollars worth of books or not. If I told you that I sold $10,000,000 worth of books at $100 each and I profited $0.01 each over the past five years working 18 hours a day, would it impress you? If you do the math, that works out to $200 per year or a wage of about $0.30 per hour. So, you can see that how many dollars worth of books I sold is irrelevant without all the other facts.

---

[1] ABE currently reports they have millions of unique customers each month visit their website and they are now operating 5 international sites.

What should be relevant to you is whether this book has any merit and whether I have sufficiently described all facets of the business should you opt to start one of your own.

If anything I will downplay the get rich quick attitude throughout this book because I am personally sick and tired of all the hyped up advertising everywhere I turn.

On television I see advertisements for the latest and greatest weight loss miracle pills or exercise gadgets during the commercial breaks of almost every show I watch. There are countless infomercials on television every night that tell me how I can get rich quick if I will only pay the three easy installment payments of $39.99 for their book of "secrets." I can tune into almost any radio station and hear similar claims, and it never ceases to amaze me that these businesses survive.

Either people are really gullible or they buy these things as some form of entertainment. I personally catalogue almost all of them as scams and the only person likely to get rich in the transaction is the seller.

I am getting a little off topic here, but I wanted to emphasize that I am not hyping anything, or promoting the online bookselling business as any kind of all inclusive solution. Like any other legitimate opportunity, there is a price to pay for success and it involves desire, commitment, and work. If you are willing to adhere to this end of the equation I do not have any doubt that you too will be successful in online bookselling. If you like books and spending time in bookstores, the business will be even more enjoyable for you and this book will help you avoid making many of the costly mistakes I made in building my business.

There are a couple other books on this subject that I have purchased and read. One of the principle reasons I decided to write a book of my own was that I wanted to cover additional topics that were not covered at all in these other books, and/or I wanted to provide more information about a specific topic that I could not find elsewhere. That is, I wanted to put out a comprehensive book on this subject that had all the hyperlinks and references at the click of a mouse because I did not think it would be very productive to buy a book and then have to type in every website address while trying to read the page of a book. Since first publishing this book in CD-ROM format, I have been convinced by customers that I should make it available in paperback as well, but alas, I have not figured out how to put hyperlinks on paper that can be accessed using a mouse. Hence, while this book in paperback may not be as efficient as the CD-ROM version, it does have the same information and more since I have made updates and revisions since the publication of the CD-ROM version. I also developed the bookkeeping software, which was not included with the CD-ROM version of the book.

Something I have made a great effort to cover in both of my book versions are detailed explanations that I have not found in any other book on this subject. I wanted it to be much more than a listing of the fundamentals with no rationale regarding the why.

I have also included some other things in this book that I have not seen in other books on this topic including some charts, graphs, and pictures to visually demonstrate the numbers or scenarios I will be describing. If a picture is really worth a thousand words, then this book is really long. My intent was not to make it long, but to make it informative, comprehensive and as interactive as possible. Along with the book I have included a CD, and on it you have been provided with some spreadsheets to help you with calculations that will make getting your online bookstore successful.

I felt a need to provide more than just text to make the book complete. I think the pictures of packing tips alone will more than save you the cost of this book in your first months of online bookselling, and I cannot imagine trying to convey these tips without pictures.

I hope you enjoy reading this book and that all of your questions are answered. If you have additional questions, please send me an email at:

mike@online-bookselling.com

and I will be happy to answer them.

# What Changed From The CD-ROM Version

After marketing this book in CD-ROM version for several months it became apparent that a paperback version was in order, owing principally to customer requests. I never intended this work to be printed because in my mind it just didn't make sense, i.e., the CD-ROM version provided almost instant access to all the websites I reference throughout the book and I cannot provide that in a paperback. Despite my best efforts to emphasize this, 80% of prospective buyers said they would prefer a paperback version that they could read anywhere and not be tied to their computer. Even though I pointed out that they could print the CD-ROM book, they still wanted a paperback. It is not my desire or intent to impose my will on others, particularly not my customers, so I have converted everything to a format suitable for print and instead of hyperlinks I have provided URL addresses.

I have also incorporated the changes that have occurred in the online marketplaces – it makes no sense to put out a new edition that does not cover the latest and greatest.

Some of the other things I have included in this edition are:

- A summary of answers to frequently asked questions.

- Instructions for using the new bookkeeping spreadsheet[2] provided with the paperback version of the book on CD.

- A discussion of how you might supplement your book sales with your own book.

- An entire section that I initially considered publishing as a stand-alone book describing how authors can get their work listed on Amazon.com without enrolling in the Amazon Connect program.[3]    This I learned by getting my CD-ROM book listed on Amazon, and although it is not difficult, Amazon.com does not make deciphering the cryptic process easy. After many hours of work and many telephone calls to Amazon, I finally figured it out. I documented the process for you to use if you decide to publish and list your own book.

I have also had a chance to get feedback from friends and customers, and this has prompted me to expand on some topics to make them easier to understand, i.e., I didn't seem to miss discussing anything in my original CD-ROM edition, but sometimes addressing a topic and making it easier to understand is more difficult to

---

[2]  I am not an attorney, bookkeeper, or licensed tax consultant. The bookkeeping spreadsheet I have included is not meant to be construed as a substitute for professional services. If you choose to use it for the tracking of your sales, expenses, and/or taxes, you should check your results and have them verified by a professional. I made every effort to assure the accuracy of the results, but using the results is based on your acceptance and you understand that I cannot be held liable for errors.

[3]  The Amazon Connect program requires an annual $30 enrollment fee and forfeiting 55% of your sales proceed to Amazon in the form of commissions.

put in writing than into speech, so I have gone through my entire book and tried to
identify any topic that needed elaboration.

# About The Author

Hello, my name is Michael (Mike) Mould and I want to introduce you to the fast-growing home-based business of selling books on the Internet. It is an evolving market with enormous potential. The amount of money you can make doing this is limited only by the amount of time you are willing to devote to it and the space you are willing to devote to an inventory. The most amazing part is how little financial investment is required, particularly if you already have an Internet connected computer and a printer. A monthly income stream of $2,000 to $4,000 is a modest expectation for someone willing to invest his or her time and energy, but don't assume it is guaranteed to make you money; it is going to require your time and effort. I do not want to discourage you in any way, it is always better to work hard - for yourself - and make money - for yourself - than it is to work hard and make someone else rich.

I have been involved in selling books through the Internet for almost five years and have thoroughly enjoyed it. I have a son that started in the business a few years before me, and it was his enthusiasm and prodding that got me started. He is a very talented musician and needed to do something that would provide him a steady and generous income while still allowing him time to write, practice, and perform his music.

His story is the classic tale of starting a business with a dollar. He literally bought his first few books with twenty dollars and sold them for considerable profit, reinvested the profit and from there things took off. Since he already had a computer and a DSL Internet connection, he never had to invest any more money in his business.

After a couple years of part-time work, his inventory was up to 5000+ books, he was making a fluctuating income of up to $10k a month, and the daily activities of his business still occupied only 2-4 hours a day. After a couple years of this and continuously hearing his stories of how well he was doing in the online bookselling business, the idea of a supplementing my own income was beginning to appeal to me more and more, so over the phone he explained how the business worked and I got started.

While I make a nice supplemental income with my online bookselling business, my profit margins are not nearly as lucrative as my son's. He is located in a part of the country that allows him to regularly attend some really great university library book sales, and over the years, he has spent considerable time and effort to educate himself with respect to what types of books do extremely well in this business.

My first experiences were disastrous and my profits were negative. I had no idea what books to buy, but I seemed to be a master at picking all the wrong ones. By the time I had 150 books that I paid $1 to $3 each for, I was just about ready to quit because they didn't seem to be selling. I seemed to be spending more on the listing fees than I was even getting for the books I sold. I was just stacking some very expensive firewood on my bookshelves.

Then, by truly dumb luck, I discovered that one of the books I had bought for $2.99 was worth $100 and I sold it within a week of listing it. Now I was really interested and asked my son come up to Washington for a few days to teach me more. He told me what types of books I should buy, how much I should pay, and where I should be looking for my inventory – some rather key pointers, don't you think? Up to that point I had been relying on instinct, i.e., buying the books I thought would be good for resale as opposed to finding out if they were good for resale before I bought them.

We spent a couple days going around on a book-hunting spree to supplement my inventory, and ended up buying 178 books in a two-day period. We listed them each evening, and one of the books he bought for $0.49 sold for $147.00 within a day! That one book paid for all the others we bought and since then, the other 177 books have brought in a profit of over $1,000. Not too bad for a weekend of book hunting. Since then I have refined my book-hunting skills and the rest is history, I am hooked. It is a fun, profitable, and educational business, but since I enjoy my career as a commercial flight test engineer, I have opted to keep my book business going as a supplemental income stream only.[4]

During the past couple years I have coached a few friends, and friends of friends, to help them get their online bookselling businesses up and going. In doing this I began to realize just how difficult it is to explain everything about the business, particularly the little nuances of daily operations, so I decided to write this book about how to sell books online so that I could capture all the little things that take so long to explain. There is nothing mentally difficult about running an online bookselling business, but there are a lot of little things that I have learned the hard and expensive way that I will be passing on to you as I have done with those I have coached.

I have chosen to continue my bookselling business as a supplemental income only because I really enjoy my day job. The online bookselling business gives my wife and I an excuse to travel[5] around to various book sales, library sales, and thrift stores in other cities to buy new inventory and allows at least part of the expenses for our travels to be deducted from our taxes as a cost of the business. All in all, it is a win-win scenario for us and we are able to locate homes for thousands of books every year.

---

[4] I have a master's degree in mechanical engineering, MSME, and work for a large commercial airplane company in Seattle, Washington as a lead engineer in Validation Instrumentation Flight Test. I am also a licensed Professional Engineer in the State of Washington.

[5] My wife is Czech, so we also like to travel to the Czech Republic frequently. Without the online bookselling business providing the nice supplemental income that it does, these trips would not happen as frequently as we like.

# Why Online Bookselling?

So, why would anyone bother selling books on the Internet? That was an easy one for me to answer for myself.

1) I like having extra money each month.

2) It was different than my career job.

3) It didn't require me to work overtime on the weekends at my regular job to have some extra spending money.[6]

4) I do most of the work associated with my online bookselling business from home.

5) The work I do have to do outside my home is done almost exclusively when I want to do it.

6) Another really nice part of having this business as a supplemental income stream is that I only do it as much as I want.

Of course, your interests are going to be different than mine, and you might even be interested in doing online bookselling as a primary source of income. There is no reason for you to not consider this, particularly if you like books, you have the space to store an adequate inventory, and you can get out enough to buy new inventory. But don't think it is going to be a no-effort endeavor it involves work and dedication.

The traditional dream of most booksellers is to open a brick and mortar storefront. This, like any other physical storefront, has inherent risks and like any other new business undertaking, the majority will fail.

Unlike opening a barbershop, which has no online competition, a brick and mortar bookstore must to some extent compete with the online dealer. I say to some extent because there is not always a direct competition for sales, i.e., there are many buyers out there that are not interested in buying a book unless they can go into the bookstore, experience the ambiance, feel and browse through the book, and then buy it from the brick and mortar store. They just seem to enjoy the experience and time spent in a traditional bookstore.

On the other hand, there are a lot of college students that buy their textbooks online exclusively so they can get a better price for their book. There are also a lot of customers that would prefer to have the book mailed to them rather than be bothered

---

[6] I have found that I can make more money working and getting paid overtime at my regular job, but I have also found that it is better for me to spend the time doing something different for income. I do not want to get burned out doing the same thing all the time and online bookselling offers me the opportunity to do something else I enjoy while still providing a substantial supplemental income.

with going to a bookstore.

Considering these two groups alone would not indicate any kind of direct competition between the online bookseller and the brick and mortar storefronts, but the tendency of the buyer to go online and have the book delivered in the mail is increasing as indicated by the sheer number of sales online. Additionally, many buyers are getting savvier and comparing prices online to those in the brick and mortar storefronts, resulting in increased online sales.

Another good reason to sell books online instead of opening a storefront is the up front investment and the operating costs of a brick and mortar storefront. Profits in book sales are high, but as soon as you lease or buy a building, hire a staff, start heating and air-conditioning the building, buy owner/occupier property and liability insurance, paying all the taxes associated with a business, and pay for all the other costs associated with having a brick-and-mortar bookstore, the profits get eaten up very quickly.

Then to top it all off, if you do find yourself closing a brick and mortar store, the closing costs associated with getting out of a lease early, liquidating your inventory at fire sale prices, legal fees, etc., are all expensive as well.

I don't want to tell you not to open your own brick and mortar store, but I do want you to be aware of the costs associated with doing it that are not incurred with an online bookstore. I also want you to know that if you decide to open a brick and mortar bookstore, you are going to find it difficult to find staff personnel that will be of much use to you, you will have to deal with employee unemployment insurance, matching Social Security taxes, federal tax reporting for employees, perhaps some form of group health/dental/vision insurance, shoplifting, employee theft, etc. A brick and mortar store also requires organizing books by subject and author which is very time consuming and expensive. Your walk-in customers are going to disorganize many books for you and you will be paying to reorganize them again. Online bookselling does not require anything more than numerically organizing your books according to when they are entered into your inventory, and as long as people in your household are not disorganizing them for you, they will be put in their place once and stay there until they are sold. Aside from the walk-in customers of a brick and mortar bookstore disorganizing your books for you, the fact that they are handling your books means that books will be damaged and the prices must be adjusted accordingly.[7]

So, you can see there are abundant reasons for considering online bookselling before you jump into that lease for a brick and mortar storefront.

---

[7] Having a customer drop a $200 book, bump the corner, or tear the dust jacket, will quite often result in you having to mark the price down as much as 85% just to sell it. Suddenly the book you paid $40 for is going to cost you money to get rid of, and it may take you a year to find someone willing to buy it damaged.

At this time it seems prudent to ask you if your ambition is to first open an online bookstore and later open a brick and mortar storefront? If this is the case, it is my belief that your goals and objectives are to progress backwards. Why on earth would you want to start a business with minimal risk, minimal cost, minimal workload, and maximized profit with the objective of moving toward maximizing risk, maximizing cost, maximizing workload while minimizing your profits?

If it is your dream to open a brick and mortar storefront, I don't want to be the one to shatter it, but I do want you to be aware that the ambition should not be attributable to profit goals, it should be attributed to other desires such as meeting your customers, a need or desire to have a physical presence in your community, or some other personal requirements. At the same time you should recognize that such a goal will most assuredly not be met with the profits that can or could be realized with an online storefront with a comparable inventory, and if profits are your ultimate objective, a brick and mortar storefront is a self-defeating goal.

In the past couple years the number of independent online booksellers has grown dramatically. This does not mean that there is not room for more, or that the competition is too stiff. Almost every time I go out searching for new books to add to my inventory I am able to come home with a book that will sell for $75 or more, a couple in the $50 range, and several that are around $20. The astonishing part is that I only frequent about 5 different places and I know there are at least a half dozen other booksellers that frequent these same places. Many of the establishments that I frequent are brick and mortar stores with clearance shelves. I have absolutely no doubt that if I chose to do so, I could make this business a full-time endeavor and make more than I make as a well-paid engineer with 20+ years of experience. There are at least 100 similar places I could buy books to add to my inventory within a 20-mile radius of my home.

Several times I have been approached by customers in the stores where I buy books and asked if I am an online bookseller, maybe they came to this conclusion because I had a shopping cart half full of books, or maybe there is something physically obvious to others that is a tell-tale sign of an online bookseller that I am unaware of. Several have told me that they tried doing the same thing but were unable to make any money doing it. I suspect their failures are owing to either a lack of interest to really make it work or a lack of the tools and tips needed to be successful. I intend to provide and describe everything you need to know to be a successful online bookseller, but I cannot provide your interest or effort, you will need to commit that part.

I don't want to mislead you, it is work and can be time consuming, but if you know the ins and outs of the business - things I will tell you about in this book - it is also very profitable. Since it has become something of a hobby to me, I do not really keep as close an eye on it as I once did, but about two years ago I kept track of the time I put into it and found I was making about $35 an hour, which is respectable, but not nearly enough for me to give up my career job.

A lot of people would love to be able to make $20 an hour from a home-based business, and the Internet book sales business is certainly one that can provide such an income, but I cannot make any guarantee that you will do this well. A lot depends on the resources you have access to for buying books, the types of books sold by these resources, and how willing you are to get out there and get seriously involved. By the same token, I don't want you to think you are bounded by a figure of $20 per hour. I previously mentioned that through Amazon.com alone there are estimated to be about $46,000 worth of books sold PER HOUR, and steadily growing. Thus, I will let you draw your own conclusion with respect to an upper bound limit for selling books online.

I am going to go in depth with respect to all facets of the online bookselling business in later chapters. Here I only wanted to point out some of the reasons for considering this type of business for you. I don't want to sound like I am hyping things up, this is not a get rich quick type of home-based business, but it is very profitable once you know what books to buy, where to sell them, how to price them, and how to get them delivered to your customers without having them get lost in the mail. Go ahead and laugh, but while the post office is a great means for sending your books to your customers, if you don't pack things and/or prepare things right, the post office will almost certainly manage to separate that book you thought was going to make you $100 profit from the envelope you shipped it in, and instead of making $100 you are going to be out $10 for the book, the postage, and the shipping envelope. I had one customer recently request that I double-wrap and double-tape the book I was shipping to her because,

> *"The post office is a minefield."*

Before we go too much farther into the online bookselling business I want you to ask yourself a few questions and reflect on your own answers.

Why do I want to sell books at all?

> Is it because you enjoy being around books, other people that read books, and spending time in bookstores? Do you enjoy buying books and having them around? Are you inclined to attach a sentimental value to books and likely to overprice them with the hope that you are forced to keep them for your own collection or can you realize the true value of a book and price it accordingly to sell?

Can you resign yourself to treat bookselling as a business rather than a hobby?

> Are you prepared to treat book buying, bookselling, and the organization of your books as a real business? Will you be able to dedicate the time needed to make a go of it as a real business, say 15 to 40 hours per week? Are you considering this undertaking as a means or excuse to add to your own collection? Some of this is comparable to the first question, but I want you to be able to draw a line between expanding a book-collecting hobby and buying books to sell.

Do you have a clear idea in your mind of what constitutes a business that is respectable, recognized and appreciated by its customers, and is oriented toward customer satisfaction?

Do you have a personality, an ambition, and a dedication to recognize the importance of customer satisfaction and a desire to strive for the goal of satisfying your customers? There are many that get into this business with the belief that they can buy books, sell them for a profit, and never consider whether the customer is happy with the book they bought. If you think this is you, think again before getting into this business. Customer feedback and returned books will almost certainly put you out of business quickly and you will be left with a large inventory of books with no marketplace that will let you list them for sale.

Do you have clear income objectives?

Before you jump off the deep end and quit your day job to sell books online think again. You need to have a plan with clear financial objectives. Are you planning on starting out small and building the business gradually? This is a realistic attitude, but before you quit your day job make sure you have considered the benefits of keeping your online bookstore as a supplemental income. For example, many day jobs provide for health insurance, which can be a substantial burden for the home-based bookstore. I just want you to be aware that before you quit your job for a short commute home-based business, the online bookstore needs to have demonstrated a track record for consistent profits that are able to absorb the additional costs you will realize when you quit your job.

Do you have the skills and business know-how to make a go of it in online bookselling?

While they are not the skills of a doctor or computer scientist, you will need to know and understand basic computer programs and how to work with the likes of a spreadsheet or database, files, folders, email, budgets, and cash flow. If you don't have these skills or knowledge, are you at least willing to learn them? You must also be prepared to spend considerable time on your computer to do such things as email customers the notification of their delivery, enter customer feedback after a sale, enter your new listings and research the going prices of you new books, process sales orders, keep records of your sales, purchases, postage, book hunting mileage, etc., so if you hate spending time on your computer this is going to be an ambitious undertaking for you. You will also need an Internet connection and some abilities to navigate the Internet.

Can you bring yourself to spend hours in bookstores and libraries every week to buy new inventory?

I don't want this to sound discouraging, but it is something that you have to enjoy doing or it will be difficult to bring yourself to do it. I spend ten to fifteen hours a week in my regular haunts looking up new books for my inventory and I love it. Since I use my cell phone to look them up using the ISBN, I try to think of it like playing a slot machine, i.e., I type in the ISBN and wait to see if I win. Sometimes I hit the jackpot, but for every book I buy I have to endure looking up ten to fifteen others that are losers. The big plus to my cell phone slot machine is that I don't have to make any investment to get a winner other than the second or two it takes to find out if I have a winner or a loser.

Do you have a back that is strong enough to carry around the books you are going to buy and sell?

I have found that the strong back is most needed when I go out to buy books for my inventory because I always seem to come back with several boxes. I personally do not have a very strong back anymore owing to an automobile accident injury, but I make up for it by packaging the books in smaller lots that I can individually carry.

Do you really have the space to store an adequate inventory?

Many that want to become online booksellers think they have the space and jump into it without really having a plan for storing their inventory or sufficient space to really store it. It takes a room about 10' x 14' to store an inventory of 3,000 books, and even then you will probably find yourself stacking books on some shelves two rows deep.

Can you bring yourself to attend garage sales, library book sales, estate sales, flea markets, thrift stores, and libraries?

Unless you plan to settle for low margin overstock lots, wholesale clearances, remainder books, or another source of inventory supply, you will need to be able to attend these events to get your inventory.

Will you be able to go through your remaining inventory on a regular basis to adjust your prices and keep your books competitive?

One of the biggest mistakes new online booksellers make is to assume that since they listed 200 books last week and have sold 50 of them, the other 150 will sell in another three weeks. Wrong! You have to stay on top of your inventory and regularly go back and re-price the ones that have not sold. I can assure you that other booksellers are regularly adding inventory too, and there will be many that will see your book listed and undercut your price. If there is a glut of new listings for a book similar to one you have listed you can bet many are undercutting your price and will sell before a buyer comes along to buy your copy. A good practice is to review as many of your old titles as the number of new listings you enter and the number of sales that you process. For example, if you just entered 50 new books in your inventory and processed

12 sales today, you should make a practice of reviewing and re-pricing 62 books today as well.

It seems apparent to me that some of the best reasons for selling used books online are owing to the nature of books themselves, i.e.:

1) Used books are easy to find.

2) The ISBN and standardization make marketing them easy.

3) Although the post office seems determined to lose or break just about anything mailed, books are not fragile and if packaged well, they do not easily escape.

4) The prices of most books are easily affordable making them easy to sell.

5) Because most books are priced less than $25, and because the online marketplaces maintain good website security, there are not many unscrupulous individuals scamming customers and making online book buying something that customers are leery about.

# What Does It Take To Get Started?

Well, it doesn't take a lot of money or any fancy equipment, but it will take a computer with an Internet connection, a printer, some books to sell, some packing supplies and tools, and a place to store the books you have for sale. Sounds simple enough, but let's discuss the need for each, and how many books is enough to get started.

## Computer and Printer

It is not necessary to have a big and powerful supercomputer, any desktop unit or laptop with Internet access will do. Like all things done on the Internet, things will go faster and with less frustration if you have a high-speed cable or DSL connection, but you can conduct this business with a dial-up connection if you do not have high-speed access.

Regarding the printer required, part of this depends on you and the records you wish to keep of this business. You may also choose to have the printer print shipping labels for you; personally, I just print the shipping information out on regular printer paper, cut the shipping address out, and tape it to the mailing envelope, but I will explain why I do this in a later chapter that details how to prepare shipments. I would suggest a laser printer with a minimum print speed of ten pages per minute, but if you are patient and wanting to start out on a shoestring budget, an ink jet printer that prints at a slower speed will suffice.

I think you will have a much better idea of the computer and printer requirements that will suit your needs after you have completed reading this book and you can envision the operation of your personal bookstore.

## Books To Sell

There is obviously not much point in opening an online bookstore with the intent of selling books if you don't have any to sell, but how many you should have to start really depends more on the type of books you have, and how quickly they will sell, i.e., the demand for the titles you want to sell. I would suggest that you obtain an absolute minimum number of 200 books, preferably 500 or more to sell before you subscribe to any of the online marketplaces because each will have subscription fees that could overwhelm any profits you might realize with too small of an inventory.[8]

I will be devoting a lot of this book to explaining how to find books, where to find books, what kinds of books to buy and what kinds not to buy, how much to pay for them, and I will even explain how you can find out what they are worth before you

---

[8] The online marketplace subscriptions start in the neighborhood of $30 per month, but you can list on Amazon free and pay 15% sales commission plus $1.00 per sale to list your books. Even this can cut into your profits quickly and I would recommend waiting until you have sufficient inventory, 200+ books, so you can justify the $39.99 per month for a Pro Merchant account on Amazon that charges the same 15% in commission, but no $1.00 per sale fee.

buy them as well as means for finding out how quickly you might expect to sell them.

## A Place To Store Your Books

It really doesn't take a lot of space to store a lot of books, but there are a few things to consider when you do your initial business planning:

1)  Plan for growth – If you are starting out with say 500 books and you decide to put them in your living room bookshelves, but you plan to grow your business to a 10,000 book inventory, you are going to need to move your books later. There are a couple problems with this.

   a. Books are heavy and not a lot of fun to move around.

   b. You risk damaging dust jackets and books every time you move them.

   c. If you don't move your books from the living room and you start storing parts of your inventory here and there throughout your house, you are going to do a lot of running around your house every day to locate the books you have sold.

   d. After 15% of the books in the living room have sold, there will be gaps in the shelves that need to be filled. If you "consolidate" your inventory by bringing books from other locations in your house you are again moving books and this will get old.

2)  Plan for keeping your books from getting damaged

   a. Don't stack your books on their covers; stand them up in the bookshelves. Stacking can cause bowing of the covers and makes it difficult to get the one on the bottom when it sells.

   b. Do not put books on the floor. Books that are put on the floor will trap moisture from the air under them and damage the bottom edge of the covers. You also risk severe damage if the room is even mildly flooded or the foundation/floor sweat (condensation).

   c. Do not put them on shelves where they are exposed to direct sunlight for any long periods of time, this will cause fading of the spines and sometimes a yellowing of the page edges.

   d. Do not put them where air conditioning vents blow directly on them. The humidity in air-conditioned air will damage them.

   e. Make sure the floor is adequately strong to support the weight of the books in the room. This is not generally a problem, but if you have any doubts about the floor, pick a different place for the shelves or have a professional review the structure for load-bearing ability.

f. Put them where children **ARE NOT** tempted to climb the shelves. This is particularly important if they start getting top-heavy. A bookcase full of books falling on an adult is dangerous; it could be fatal for a child.

g. Store them for easy access. You are going to be locating books to ship regularly and it is not fun to sell a book and not be able to find it to ship.

A little common sense and planning will go a long way toward making the operation of your online bookstore safe, easy, profitable, and enjoyable to run.

Getting started is not difficult and the financial investment in minimal, particularly if you already have an Internet connected computer and a printer. Purchasing your initial inventory and subscribing to an online marketplace are the only other investments you really need to make to get started. If you don't have bookshelves, you can buy some cinderblocks and 2 x 6's and make shelves from them, but if you do this, please make sure the kids are kept away from them, these shelves are particularly susceptible to collapse if children start climbing them.

Above is an example of the 2" x 6" x 8' board and cinderblock shelves I built to store my inventory.

To give you an idea of the space required I will describe how I stored 2,500 books in a 10' x 10' extra bedroom quite handily. I put bookshelves (2' x 3' x 6') all around the walls and one unit 2' x 3' x 6' in the center of the room. I stood the books up, two rows deep on each shelf (except for the top and bottom shelves), and was able to easily access books sold each day. Hint: Now that my inventory is over 2,500 books I have had to set up my inventory in another part of my house and move all those books. That is why I emphasized to "Plan for Growth," I didn't, and moving all those books was not fun.

I will also tell you that the shelves I used in this room were purchased at a home improvement store for about $50 per unit. They are the heavy-duty plastic units with PVC pipe legs between the shelves. Initially I used the cheaper $30 units, but I had one collapse from the weight of the books, and when it fell, it crippled the leg of an adjacent unit and caused it too to collapse. That was an incident for which I have no excuse. I am a licensed professional mechanical engineer and I could see the legs of these shelves bowing under the weight of the books. I knew it was inevitable that they would collapse from a compression buckling failure of the legs, but I also knew it was going to be a lot of work to unload the shelves and restack the books on new shelves. The collapse not only destroyed the shelf units, several of the books were damaged and I had to reduce the prices of the damaged books accordingly.

So you see, there is good reason for a little planning, not only for how big you might want to grow your bookstore, but for using adequate storage facilities – books are heavy, just pick up a box full of them and then reflect on how many boxes of books a typical book shelf can hold.

**Once again I want to emphasize safety and the fact that books are heavy. A bookshelf full of books is not a safe thing for a child to climb. If it topples over on top of a child, it could cause severe injury or even death, so please consider the danger and if you have any doubts, store your books where your children do not play.**

## Other Tools And Supplies

There are some basic tools and supplies you will need, including:

Scissors
2" cellophane tape
Tape dispenser
2" stretch & shrink-wrap
Clean newsprint wrapping paper (I use 24" x 36" torn in half)
Bondo® blade or similar squeegee for running bubbles out from under tape
Goo Gone® (or similar label adhesive remover and cleaner)
Return address stamp for your business
Assorted sizes of self-sealing bubble packs (I stock #0, #1, #2, #3, #4, #5, & #6)
10" x 13" envelopes
A quality soft eraser (I use a white drafting quality eraser)
Sharpie® pens (black and red)
Large Glue Stic®
Small plastic scraper (to scrape off price stickers)

# What Constitutes Successful?

This is a business that requires minimal investment and offers some lucrative returns, but what really constitutes successful?

What would you think of an investment that offers a return of 250% annually? What would you think of a business that allowed you to return a profit of 400% to 29,900% on individual items you sold? These numbers are not fiction!

In the past three years I have realized a profit of over 250% on the total inventory I have purchased with an average profit of over 320% on the books I have sold. I even had several books sell for profits exceeding 5000% with one exceeding 88,000%. Imagine buying a book for $0.49 and selling it for $147.00 in two days. That is 29,900% profit, and that is exactly what I did. I admit that this kind of return on investment is not that common, but I regularly buy books for a dollar the sell for more than $50.00 and you can too.    Just this week I sold a book to the United Nations for $260.04 that I purchased for $0.25. That is a profit of 88,314% *after* paying the Amazon.com sales commission!

I have a son in this business that bought seven shopping carts full of books at a university library book sale for just over $500. Just three days later, one of the books in his purchase sold for over $750.00. The sale of that one book alone brought him a profit of over $250, after paying for the rest of the books he bought, giving him an inventory of over six hundred books that were all paid for by selling just one book. Since then, he has profited over $6,000 from the sale of other books purchased at that one sale.

That is good business and he only does this a few hours a week. Granted, not all such book sales are this lucrative, but if you learn to be a savvy book buyer, they are almost all profitable. If you don't learn the ropes, chances are you will be buying a bunch of very expensive firewood. That is why I have put together this book to help you be successful. To give you an idea of the profits you can anticipate, the actual numbers from the last 3,000 books I have sold are:

Average Selling Price:     $ 6.95
Average cost:              $ 1.64

Average profit (excluding postage reimbursement profits):  $ 5.31

And I make on average another $0.24 per book from the postage reimbursements.

When was the last time you invested in something that returned 320% regularly? If you have a system that did return 320% on a regular basis, I doubt you would be looking into this business. I want to emphasize that 320% profit is a reasonable expectation for anyone that gets actively involved in this business, but to be successful you will need to invest the time to become proficient at picking books to resell and you will need to invest some money to purchase an inventory. In most cases, the time investment will be on the order of 10-15 hours per week to maintain an inventory of about 2,000 books, and a financial investment of approximately $3,000 for the books and supplies needed to conduct the business. Of course, you don't have to have this kind of inventory right out of the gate, nor do you have to invest $3,000 right up front, you can use the profits from a smaller initial inventory to build up to this, in fact, if you have between 200 and 500 books initially, that will get you started – if and only if they have a resale value, and your up front investment will be on the order of $500 to $800 if you already have the computer and printer. In the long run, your initial investment should be your only out-of-pocket investment as all of the rest of the books you add to your inventory should come from the profits from selling books.

So, what does it take to become a successful used bookseller? First, lets establish what we mean by successful, and not just in terms of dollars per month because this can be misleading. If you are going to sell used books there are several things you have to consider before establishing what constitutes being successful.

It is important to decide if this is something you want to do as a supplemental income, or whether it is something you want to do as a sole income. If you are considering used book sales as a supplemental income you can probably get by with a much smaller inventory and certainly a much smaller investment. As a rule of thumb I have found that I can profit about $0.75 per month for each book I have in my inventory. Thus, for an inventory of 1000 books I can expect to profit about $750 per month, which would be a nice supplemental income for most and would imply that you could make a similar amount of money each month if you maintain an inventory of 1000 books. Since I have been doing this for quite some time, it would be better for you to estimate your profits to be on the order of $0.50 per book in your inventory, and only that much once you have eliminated the books that have a firewood value. It does take time and experience to learn which books to put in your inventory to sell.

For example, most of the novels you see that have been out for a couple years have an online resale value of $0.01 and I would not even bother putting them in my inventory, they have only a firewood value. I will tell you a lot more about how to select books for resale later, right now I just want to point out that just because you have an inventory of 10,000 books does not mean you can expect to make $7,500 per month selling them, in fact, if you just went out and bought up 10,000 books without knowing whether or not they had any resale value, you would probably make about $75 per month selling them. I can speak to this from experience because when I first started I bought books that I thought would sell without knowing or researching their value. Consequently, I bought a lot of expensive firewood as I explained before.

You should also be aware that it does require time to run a used book business on-line. You have to buy books, research prices. Enter the books into a database, upload new books to your online seller program, process daily book orders, clean the books before packing them, address the packages, and my least favorite part of the business is the standing in line at the post office.

As you gain experience at each of these tasks, the per book time spent doing them will reduce substantially, each that is except for the post office part. Nothing you do will make the post office experience any less painful, but if you are lucky, you can pick a time of day to take your books to the post office when they are not too busy. It never fails, when I show up at the post office to ship books, there is a line of at least 25 people and only one postal clerk working, but if I do not need any help and stop in the post office to check my box, there is nobody in line and there are at least four clerks working.

You will have to put time into this business and depending on how much you want to make, you will have to decide just how much time and money you want to invest. It can be very lucrative if you have the time, money, and interest to invest in learning all the facets of the business, but if your interest is only a curiosity, your time is very limited, and you have very little money to invest, chances are your used book selling business will turn into a hobby of collecting books.

If you are still with me here, I am assuming that you are interested in getting your own used book selling business started, so I want to tell you what a typical week in the business is like, and some of the tasks you will be doing on a less frequent basis.

Every day, seven days a week, you will process orders you receive through your bookseller program. This amounts to going online, reviewing the orders placed, accepting and/or rejecting the orders, printing the mailing instructions and invoices for each, updating your inventory database, and uploading the database updates to your online bookseller program. You will also pull the books you sold from your shelves, clean them up (remove price stickers, erase prices written inside covers, clean dust jackets) and package them (bubble wrap envelopes). Then you will address the envelopes and in some cases, you will need to weigh the package, fill out confirmation/tracking paperwork, customs forms, and/or insurance forms.

At least three times a week you will need to visit your sources for buying books to add to your inventory. How often you need to do this will depend greatly on how many books you are selling and whether or not you are making as much as you want to make. If you are selling 75 books a week and you are satisfied with how much money you are making, then you will need to buy comparable books at the rate of 75 per week to maintain your inventory and the level of income you are satisfied with. If you are only making $100 per week and selling 200 books a week, but you want to make $150 per week, then you need to be buying books of comparable resale value faster than you are selling them so that your quantity in inventory goes up and hence your sales volume will increase. In any case, unless you are just trying to sell out your inventory and shut down your business, you will need to get out and buy books as fast as you sell them.

Once a week you will need to assess your inventory of books to know how many you started the week with and whether or not you need to buy more. You will also need to check your supplies, e.g., bubble envelopes, priority mailers, tape, printer paper, postal forms, etc.[9]

---

[9] This is a task that many online booksellers overlook or forget to do, until they run out of self-sealing bubble pack envelopes and have to buy some from the local office supply store instead of buying them in bulk. If you forget this and pay up to ten times as much for these envelopes at an office supply store, you will learn to check your supply inventory regularly, or you will find yourself losing a lot of money on shipping.

Once a month, or each two months, you will need to review the pricing of your remaining inventory. Since the predominate trend for all booksellers listing new copies of books is to list at lower prices than others currently listing, in many cases you will find that your books that have been listed for some time, but haven't sold, are no longer competitively priced. This can be a very time consuming process if you have a large inventory, but if you do not keep your books competitively priced, they may never sell.

I suspect you are wondering why I am willing to share the secrets of my successful online book selling business with you knowing this could lead to more competition for me. The answer is two-fold and really quite simple. First of all, this book constitutes one of approximately fifty CD books that I sell, and none of them cost me much of anything but time to create and/or market. Since this book is the only e-book I have in my inventory that could indirectly cost me in any way, I am not about to give it away, i.e., it is $39.99 for the following reasons:

1) I have spent a lot of time writing it.

2) If there is a risk that it might cost me in the long run to divulge the information, I would like to make something from the dissemination of the information

3) There is no shortage of supplies with respect to used books.

4) If you buy books and sell them, there will still be countless numbers of people donating their used books to thrift stores and libraries that I and others can buy from, so I doubt that competing with you is going to put me out of business.

5) If you are going to be an online bookseller, it is to my benefit that you are taught how to do it with integrity so that customers of yours are satisfied with their online book purchase, i.e., it is detrimental to the online bookselling business to have booksellers that do not satisfy their customers to the point that the customer will not make future online book purchases.

Another reality is that despite me selling you all of this information, I doubt more than one in twenty buyers is actually going to actively pursue the opportunity and/or build an inventory that will compete with mine. Regardless of the facts and the potential rewards, few people will go to the trouble, or effort.

Thus, you can see that "successful" is an arbitrary term that means something different to every person. If you want to supplement your income with $500 a month, that should be very easy, but if you want to sell books online for a living and make $10,000 a month, it is doable, but it is going to take time, money, and effort to build up to that level.

Now that you have a very broad overview of the business I want you to reflect on your own interpretation of "successful" and establish a realistic goal for yourself and your online bookselling business.

# Dedication, Time, and Patience

This is not a get rich quick endeavor, and unless you get really lucky in your first inventory purchases, you are not likely to realize big profits immediately. That said, there is no reason not to expect immediate profits that grow steadily as you build your inventory and increase your sales.

The three keys to developing a successful Internet bookselling business are dedication, time, and patience and I would like to address each of these to eliminate confusion and convey what I mean.

## Dedication

You cannot go out and buy 500 books, list them, and then just sit back and wait for the profits to roll in. Purchasing inventory is an ongoing task that you must actively continue doing if you want to continue selling online. The more books you have of value, the more you will sell, but if you sell a book you now have one less book available to sell and a diminished probability of additional sales. All books are not created equal and those with the highest demand will typically sell first, leaving you with a remaining inventory that is in less demand. There are tools I will discuss later that will help you understand the consumer demand for your books, but I want to make it clear to you here that every time you sell a book, those left in your inventory are in lower demand. Thus, to keep your inventory demand up you need to keep up your inventory and that means dedicating yourself to continually seeking additional inventory.

## Time

The aspect of time is particularly important when you are just getting started, but it should also be clear that although you will get better at conducting this business and your efficiency will improve, there would not come a point where you do not need to spend time on this business. Before you jump into launching your Internet bookselling business make sure you have at least 20 hours a week to carry out the business with at least two hours a day every day. You might be wondering why you can't just dedicate two ten-hour sessions on Saturday and Sunday to get things done instead of spreading everything out through the week. Well, when you start selling online you are going to learn that you cannot wait to send the books your customers order, they need to be prepared and shipped daily. On the weekends you may find yourself at book sales or in thrift shops looking for new inventory.

The long and the short of it is that this is a real business and it does take time to build and operate.

## Patience

Don't expect to make $10k the first month with only 500 books listed; it is not going to happen. Pace yourself and remain determined to build your business steadily, before you realize what happened it is quite likely that you will have a few thousand books and find yourself making a few thousand dollars a month.

You will also need to exercise patience in finding your inventory. It is not very likely that you are going to walk into the first thrift store you try and purchase a thousand books for $20 that will sell online for $100k.

There are a lot of online booksellers out there already and chances are that they are frequenting your local bookstores and thrift shops for inventory too. At the same time, do not let this discourage you. In my small town I am aware of at least six other serious online booksellers and I see them regularly at the places I buy books. That doesn't stop me from checking these places for inventory, but it does motivate me to check these places more frequently because I know the stores are constantly adding books to their shelves. I also know that many times I can walk into a thrift store immediately after one of my competitors has left and still find a few hundred dollars worth of books that they either missed, did not have the experience or tools to recognize as having value, or did not bother to check.

One such experience I will share with you to demonstrate exactly what I am trying to convey. A few years ago when my youngest son was visiting, we went to a thrift store that I knew was regularly checked by several online booksellers. We had about 75 books in our shopping cart that we were purchasing for my inventory and a man that was just getting started in online bookselling approached me. I was sitting on a ledge in the store checking the last few prospective books we thought might be of value and this man started a conversation with me. In our discussion he told me that he thought the store was picked clean and he never seemed to be able to find any books of value from their stock, but he saw that I had a bunch in my shopping cart and wondered how I identified them. As I was talking with him I looked up at a book at the end of a row just across the aisle from me, and since I had never seen it before (*The Golfer and the Millionaire: It's About Having the Drive to Succeed*, by Mark Fisher) I decided to grab it and check it out. While I was talking with him I looked this book up and found that it sold in very good condition for $99 on Amazon.com, and this particular copy looked brand new. So, for $0.49 I bought the book and told him the value. He told me that he came in there regularly with his note pad and wrote down ISBN numbers, titles, etc., then went home to look them up on his computer and if they had any value he would come back and buy them. You know, there are a lot of online sellers that do this and since there are sellers like me that look books up on their cell phones, I am sure these dealers miss out on a lot of valuable books. It is far too time consuming to write down a bunch of book information, drive home, look the books up, and then go back to the store to see if the ones of value are still there, so I will be telling you how to look them up to know their value while you are still in the store.

The point is that there are very few online booksellers that will walk into any store and walk out with all the books of value. I was in the library a while back and thought I had gone through the sale shelf very thoroughly when another dealer came in and pulled a book from the same shelf I had just checked. The book was selling in the library for a quarter and on Amazon.com it was selling for $154. I missed it!

If you are patient, as well as persistent, you will find books that will make you a nice profit even if other dealers are buying their inventory from the same places as you.

# Is There A Future In Online Bookselling?

I guess only the future will be able to answer this question, but my bet is that there is a future in this business. In fact, I am still investing in it regularly and so are a lot of other online booksellers. I also believe that it is and will continue to become more competitive, but I am still able to find valuable books and I am still making money doing it.

The logical question for you to ask here is why am I publishing a book that will create more competition for myself; one that could diminish my probability of success? This is a question that I have been asked several times by prospective customers of the CD-ROM book version. It is a good question with simple answers and warrants some elaboration on my earlier answers.

- This is just one more book in my inventory to sell, and regardless how many people buy this book there will still be people donating books to their local libraries and thrift stores that they must sell to stay in business. Sure, some libraries are now marketing the donated books in much the same way I am, but they have limited space and when they don't sell or they cannot get enough volunteers to list them, they still put them out on clearance shelves. My own local branch is regularly criticized by the Fire Marshall for having too many books stacked in their back room, and he has told to clear them out.

- The statistician in me reminds me that despite the number of people that buy this book, only a small percentage will actually put the principles to practice and of those that do, few will operate an online bookstore with an inventory that competes with mine. There are literally millions of book titles out there, and if you are looking for unusual titles as I will explain later are the most profitable, the chance of us both having more than a few duplicate titles is small, even if we both have an inventory of 10,000 books. I will illustrate this by discussion.

  Suppose you and I both have an inventory of 10,000 books and that there were only 100,000,000 unique book titles ever printed. Further, suppose that neither of us has more than one copy of any given title. Than means that each of us has 10,000 of the 100,000,000 titles ever printed, or 0.01%. The probability of us having even a couple titles that are the same is small, and the probability of us having many titles that are the same is even smaller.

  The reality is that since we will both be buying books that are more modern, the number of available titles is a much smaller number and the probability of us having several books with the same titles is good, but on the whole, our inventories will differ substantially.

- If I can teach online booksellers to operate their businesses professionally, there will be more satisfied customers buying books online and that is better than having everyone open an online bookstore and operating it in a haphazard fashion that ultimately turns people away from buying online.

There are billions of books all over the world and people ready to donate them. There are also millions of buyers out there looking for many of those books. I doubt the business is going to diminish any time soon. A good indication of the health of the market is Amazon.com, BarnesandNoble.com, Half.com, Abebooks.com, and slews of other lesser-known online marketplaces. They are growing businesses, which means more and more people are buying and selling books over the Internet.

I have been involved in online bookselling for almost five years and have experienced nothing but growth. If another twenty people in my own town start doing this too, it will be a bit tougher to buy books for my inventory, but I am sure my dedication, time and patience commitments will enable me to keep the business flourishing.

When online bookselling first began, the big publishing houses, the national bookstore chains, and book authors were outraged and raised a big ruckus claiming Amazon.com was going to put them out of business by making used books readily available at cheap prices. Well, it did force the publishers and chain bookstores to be more efficient, but people still go to the brick and mortar book stores and buy books. Some of the big publishing houses have or are implementing print on demand technology. This will make online bookselling more competitive since new books will get cheaper, but I doubt it will bring an end to online bookselling. People and businesses are adaptable and the dynamics of the industry will no doubt require changes, but none of the big online marketplaces are cutting back on their growth and I do not intend to devote much attention to it until I see them making changes that indicate a negative growth in the industry.

In summary, my personal opinion is that indeed there is a future in online bookselling. The overall scenario is one of dynamic growth and the industry is still in its infancy.

There are as many predictions about the future of online bookselling as there are book buyers and booksellers; thus, your prediction is no better than mine or that of another experienced bookseller, except that I and other experienced booksellers can speak to the trends we have seen. It is getting more competitive, there does not seem to be any shortage of resources for finding and buying inventory, the number of online buyers is dramatically increasing daily, and without a doubt it will at some point normalize and settle down with respect to the number of online booksellers.

If you start your own online bookselling business and establish yourself well, there is no reason not to believe that you can be a part of the "normalized" number of those that survive.

# Where To Buy Your Inventory

If you stop and think about it I am sure you could come up with every resource I am going to tell you about and maybe even more, but I want to also tell you about some "insider" considerations that you probably don't know.

## Local Library Fundraising Shelves

In my part of the country, these shelves are run by the *Friends of the Library* and the books sold are those that are donated directly to that library by its patrons.

This is one of my favorite places to buy books because they are priced to move. Most hardcover books are a dollar, and many paperbacks are only a quarter. I cannot tell you how many books I have purchased from my local branch library for a dollar and sold for $50 to $150. You might wonder why the library doesn't just sell them online and raise more funds. I cannot say for sure, but I suspect a lot of it has to do with the number of volunteers, how much space they have to store the books, the logistics of packing and shipping the books they sell, and possibly the charity nature of the fundraising group itself. At the same time, there are a number of library systems nationwide that are beginning to sell online; they are realizing just how much more they can get for some of the donated titles than the *Friends of the Library* sales shelves will bring them. This is bad news for online booksellers that rely on these fundraising shelves for inventory, but libraries may start realizing a reduction in the number of patrons willing to donate books when the patrons learn of the business and profit nature of the "Friends" organizations. They may also realize an IRS change in their charity status when the IRS sees the profits being generated by these organizations, or a reduction in the federal and state library funding when these governments realize the funds the libraries generate through donation sales. In the past few months I have seen my local branch jacking up the prices of the books on the *Friends* shelves. I suspect a lot of this is owing to their recognition that I and other booksellers keep coming back to buy their books, which in turn means we must be making some good money from their books. The result has been that their shelves are now very full because we are not willing to pay these inflated prices, and in the past month, the prices have started coming down again. The plain and simple truth is that they do not have the space to store the books being donated and if they don't sell the books on their *Friends* shelves, they will have to throw the books away because the Fire Marshall is not going to overlook the piles in the back room.

At one time I offered to deposit a dollar a book and sell the books for the library on a consignment basis if they would let me go through them prior to putting them out for sale. I was told they could not do this without violating the law with respect to their charity nature.[10]

---

[10] One customer of my CD-ROM book was able to set up just such a consignment arrangement with his local *Friends of the Library* organization, so I think the rejection I got from my library is owing to a snooty librarian or library board member that is opposed to online bookselling.

In any case, if you do decide to use your library as a resource for your inventory, visit their sale shelves **frequently**. Since these shelves are kept organized and stocked by volunteers with sporadic schedules, they can be stocked any time of any day the library is open. If you live in a large city you can also anticipate that other booksellers are also visiting these *Friends of the Library* shelves to stock their inventory too, so frequent visits are more likely to get you more books. I visit my library so frequently that a number of other dealers have given up trying to find any books for their inventory, in fact, about a month ago, I met one of my competitors as I was leaving the library and as soon as he saw that I was leaving he turned around and left because he knew I didn't leave anything worth his time to look through the library's shelves.

In the past I would see this particular dealer about once a week, but since the day he turned around and left I have not seen him at all, and since then I have purchased a few hundred books from the same library. Perhaps he too has given up this library as a source for his inventory and my persistence has paid off.

Another thing to keep an eye out for when buying from the library fundraising shelves is their pricing. There does not seem to me to be any logic applied when they price their books to sell. I have purchased many books for a quarter that are worth well over a hundred dollars and I have seen books priced for $15 that sells on Amazon.com for a penny. It is best not to blindly buy, but to know what a book is worth before you buy it. I will be discussing some ways you can do this later in this book.

## Community Book Sales

This type of sale is also known as a neighborhood yard sale and can have many treasures. Personally, I do not attend many of these sales. Not because they do not have good books, but because I have several other sources that keep me stocked and busy. Although I do not frequent them, I have been to a few and found books that are worth purchasing for resale. Most of these sales will price books at fifty cents for a hardback and a quarter for a paperback, and most of those for sale are worthless for resale. On occasion you will come across one that has a bunch of textbooks that someone used in college. The fact that they are textbooks does not alone mean that they are worth buying, but they do merit checking out.

At a sale like this if you see some books that you already know are worth buying and some that you suspect might be worth buying but do not have the time to look them up, you might try making an offer to purchase a lot, say fifty, for $20 if they are selling for fifty cents each. Too many times I have purchased books that I thought would be good sellers without spending the time to look them up first, now I won't buy a book for more than a quarter unless I look it up first. My mistakes comprise about a cord of firewood at a cost of thousands of dollars. Fortunately, I have learned to identify winners much better and have added very few logs to the firewood pile in the past 3-1/2 years.

## Church Fundraisers

A church fundraiser is generally better than a community book sale because for some reason people are more reluctant to donate their garage collections of junk to their church sales than a community sale, i.e., they seem to be embarrassed to give junk to their church, but not to the neighborhood. Other aspects of the church fundraiser are similar and you can similarly make offers for a lot of books at a reduced price.

If you go to a church fundraiser sale that has a lot of elderly among the church's congregation, you are also likely to find some real treasures because the elderly tend to be more generous in their church donations and many of them donate books they have had in their personal collections for many years.

## Thrift Stores

This is another of my favorite haunts, but because they typically price their books higher than many other sources I am more selective about the books I buy in thrift stores.

Most of the thrift stores around me price hardbacks at $2.99 and paperbacks at $1.99, so I need to feel there is sufficient profit to be had when I invest in buying these books and I need to know that the book is in demand. It doesn't mean a thing to buy a book worth $250 if there is no demand for it and nobody is going to buy it – unless you just want to keep it for yourself.

There is a tool out there that will in most cases help you to understand what the demand for a book is, and like the tool I mentioned for determining the value of a book I will address it later.

## Book Store Clearance Shelves

This source is right behind the local library as my second favorite place to buy books. There are a number of chain bookstores across the country that have clearance shelves in their stores.

The clearance shelves are stocked regularly with all sorts of valuable books. You might wonder why these stores would put these books on their clearance shelves if they have a substantial value, and that is a good question.

The chain that is close to my home buys books, CD's, records, etc., from anyone that brings them in. They will sort through them and put the ones they think they can sell in their store on their shelves, the rest go on the clearance shelves or off to donation. They also put books on their clearance shelves that have dropped in demand or that they overstocked.

Just because the books have dropped in demand sufficiently to warrant the bookstore putting them on the clearance shelf does not mean you can't sell them for a profit on the Internet. Remember, the demand within their store is limited to the people that walk in the door; the demand over the Internet constitutes millions of potential buyers every day. Most bookstores are lucky to see a million potential customers in the lifetime of the store.

I have never gone to the clearance shelves of the bookstore in my neighborhood and failed to leave with books to add to my inventory. Many times they are textbooks that have minor highlighting that perhaps the store does not feel are in good enough condition to put on their shelves. If I list a book with highlighting, I state it in the listing, but this does not seem to faze many buyers and quite often what the bookstore does not feel is good enough for their shelves will make me $50. Unless a book is in really bad condition, the cover is falling off, or all the pages have separated from the binding, it will probably sell as a used book if you are honest about the condition and price it accordingly.

I have also found books in my local bookstore that are in mint condition for a dollar that I have sold for $125. I do not know if this was put on their clearance shelves by mistake, or if they just felt it was something they could not sell, but as long as they put out books of value I will continue buying from their clearance racks.

On a couple occasions I mentioned to the staff in this store that they had some really valuable books on their clearance racks and was told that they just had too many copies to keep them all, or they were overwhelmed with used books.

Since I felt an obligation to tell them, and I did, I have not made it a point of discussion with them anymore. I also do not feel too bad getting a good deal from them after seeing what they pay their customers for used books. I remember watching them unload a couple boxes of books brought in by one customer in an area I could access, and there were books in those boxes that made the total value in excess of $600. They bought the entire lot for $12. Apparently, people that sell their books by the box don't really care what they get for the books; they just want some space on their shelves.

Another reason for finding such valuable books on their clearance shelves might be owing to an inadequately trained staff, i.e., they may not know how to determine a book's value or they may not even care if they can't find it the first place they look. This could also be a reason for you to reflect and reconsider any plans you might have for opening a brick and mortar store.

It was from my local chain bookstore that I bought *Kate: The Kate Moss Book*, by Kate Moss for $0.90 and sold for $199.99, and many of the other gems I have listed on my website.

## Book Store Bargain Tables

These are very similar to the clearance shelves in bookstores, but are almost always comprised of strictly new books that the bookstore overstocked.

Be careful when buying from the bargain tables, the books are not always a bargain – at least from the perspective of one that would like to resell them.

Quite frequently these tables have a bunch of coffee table picture books and this type of book generally does not have much resale value.

## Estate Sales

This source comes in third on my favorites list, but not because randomly attending an estate sale is a good way to find books for my inventory.

I like estate sales because I have been able to establish a synergistic relationship with some of the estate liquidators that allow me to preview the books being liquidated in the estate for a percentage of the ultimate profits. I have a relationship with one liquidator that purchases all of the books I identify as having a resale value and then on a consignment basis I sell them for him. Initially I was a little concerned about the ethics of doing this, but we consulted an attorney representing the estate and we were informed that as long as he was paying what was being asked for the books in the estate liquidation everything would be fine. Thus, the liquidator generally pays a dollar a piece for the hardbacks I identify and seventy-five cents for the paperbacks. I then market the books and give him a percentage of the sales profits. It has turned out to be lucrative for both of us.

There are other estate sales that are worth going to and buying entire collections, but before making an offer to do so; you better have a good idea what the collection is worth. I typically treat all estate sales as I would a garage sale with respect to books.

If you cannot find an estate liquidator that will allow you to preview and purchase books from the estate he/she is liquidating, you may be able to establish a relationship with him/her whereby you can purchase the leftover books at a very cheap price because once the sale ends, the remnants of the estate sale are many times just donated to a thrift store or charity and if the estate liquidator has to move them to donate them, he/she might be happy to have you haul them away at a cheap price.

One final thing to suggest is that you have business cards made for your online bookselling business so you can leave one with the estate liquidator when you express an interest in establishing a synergistic relationship with him/her and/or if you suggest you might be interested in buying all of the books remaining after the estate sale is finished.

## Garage Sales

Many garage sales have books for sale and I have purchased many books from them, but the quantity of books is generally quite small and the cost to drive around and pick up a couple books here and there is just not worth the quantities of books available.

If you browse your local classified advertisements and run across an garage sale that specifically mentions books, and if it lists a phone number, it might be worth your time to make a phone call and ask how many books they are selling and of what type. If the quantity is large, or if the books are of a type (more about this later) that sell well, it might be worth attending, otherwise I would limit my garage sale attendance to those I see when I am out doing something else and happen to pass by.

## Newspaper Classified Advertisements

There is the odd advertisement selling large quantities of books that is worth checking out. Typically these advertisements are business liquidations and require local pickup rather than shipping, so you are limited to advertisements in your local newspaper.

## Wholesale Remainder Distributors

This is not really a suggested source for the bookseller just getting started. You really need to have some experience when buying from a wholesaler that is selling remainders because you typically have minimum purchase requirements for any particular title as well as a minimum total order requirement.

These distributors are selling these books cheap for a reason, the market has been saturated nationwide and there isn't much demand for these books anymore.

I have bought a few $500 minimum orders from such distributors, and I made out okay, but I did not recover my investment for almost nine months and the total profit margin has never approached the margins I realize from my other favorite sources.

After you have been buying and selling books for a couple years and have a really good sense for what will sell and what will not sell, it might be worth your time to start checking out some wholesale distributors of remainder books, until then think of them as slow sellers or firewood.

I have provided a list of wholesalers and remainder distributors for you, but this is of such little worth to you right away that it merits only an Appendix reference. Remember, the profit potential on remainders and wholesale purchased books is marginal and sales are very competitive, you will realize much greater per book profits from books you buy at library book sales, estate sales, thrift stores, and in many cases even garage sales.

If you bought this book hoping to get a "secret" list of wholesale or remainder book distributors I apologize for the hype other authors have given this source. I have made it abundantly clear in my advertising that I have included an exhaustive list of wholesale and remainder book distributors, but there is nothing secret about them and a quick Google search will reveal most of the available distributors. I am aware of other authors that advertise such secret or exclusive lists, and I have their books too. What is secret or exclusive about information that is readily available to the general public? It is just hype and you should steer clear of all of these distributors until you really know what you are doing in online bookselling.

## Bulk Lots On eBay.com

This is really dangerous ground for a novice. All of the bulk lot auctions sound great, but many of them are the firewood that has been weeded out of the inventories of other online booksellers. Certainly there are some legitimate auctions of bulk lots, but they are few and far between.

After about three years of selling online, my youngest son needed to clear out his inventory to do some work on his house and he put up 2000 books on eBay.com in a bulk lot with a reserve. The first time his auction ran, his reserve was not met and he figured this was because nobody could see what books he had, so he put a file in his auction that listed the books he was selling and their ISBN numbers. This time the reserve was met and surpassed, and a buyer drove about 150 miles to pick up the inventory. The reality is that he got about 15% of the online value, but substantially more than his investment, and the buyer got a great deal on 2000 books for his online inventory.

If you can find such an auction and verify the value of the inventory being sold – great – if not, don't be surprised if you end up buying a $2,000 cord of firewood.

If you are going to consider buying bulk lots on an eBay.com auction, first contact the buyer and ask for a list of the books, their ISBN numbers, or at least the titles and authors so that you can do some research. If the buyer cannot provide this it would probably be best to steer clear, particularly if the auction states that it is the inventory of an online dealer going out of business or a bookstore closing. These statements in conjunction with an inability to provide an inventory listing should set off all kinds of bells and whistles warning you to stay away.

There are now a number of professional auction services nationwide that do run legitimate bulk sales of all kinds of things, including books. One I am aware of has an arrangement with a bankruptcy trustee that allows them to liquidate bankruptcy estates for the trustee. In this case I would not hesitate to bid on a bulk lot of books they were auctioning because I know they have not gone through them and picked out all the winners first. They simply do not have the time or resources to be bothered and are offering a legitimate lot of possibly valuable books.

Before you start bidding on bulk lots of books offered in eBay.com auctions, do a little research. If you don't, you are likely to pay a thousand dollars for a few pallets of firewood.

## Auctions

There are a number of auctions, usually estate auctions, which offer book lots. The advantage to this type of auction as opposed to an eBay.com auction is that there is generally a preview period where you can look at the books or other merchandise being auctioned.

If you plan to bid at an auction, attend the preview and do some research. You might even consider taking a digital camera and a few pictures at the preview to help you remember the titles you want to research before the auction itself.

The research you do will give you a good idea of the maximum that should be paid for the books and what you might expect in the way of a profit. It will also give you some idea of how long it might take to recover your investment.

There are probably going to be other very knowledgeable booksellers at the auction that have a lot of experience at buying lots of books like this. Don't let your enthusiasm get the best of your good judgment.

## Book Fairs And/Or Library Book Sales

A book fair and a library book sale are very similar events, with the library book sale usually being a bigger event. It is usually a great opportunity to buy a large quantity of books for your inventory, but there usually isn't much time to research or check prices, so it is better to start attending them after you have more experience.

Both events usually have what is called a preview sale. It is usually held a day or two before opening to the general public and an admission is usually charged to attend the preview sale. Speaking from experience, I would recommend attending the preview sale because there will be a number of other online booksellers attending and they will certainly pick through the available books to buy the winners they can identify.

If you go to a book sale preview sale, **DO NOT BE LATE!** If you aren't there when the doors open, you are going to miss out on a lot of available books as other online booksellers are going to grab them up quickly.

Both events are usually fast-paced with people quickly going through the available books and putting them in boxes to buy. There is one type of buyer that is particularly annoying, the one that hoards books only to slink off into a corner and check values so he/she can purchase only those with respectable resale values. Many of the library book sales I have attended prohibit such behavior and I would like to see it adopted across all such sales.

When you attend one of these events, be sure to take along several boxes to put the books you want in. You should also have your name clearly marked on your boxes ahead of time so that other buyers know you intend to purchase the books you have put in the boxes and that the boxes are not just additional resources that would not fit on the tables or shelves. Some sales have a holding area for you to put your filled boxes in so that this does not happen, but I usually just take my wife along to guard the boxes I have filled.

The last such event I attended resulted in me buying 173 books for $154. After three weeks I recovered my investment and after another three months I realized a profit of over $600 and still had about 130 of the original 173 books in my inventory. It has taken about a year to dwindle the books bought at that sale down to about 50, but the profit is now up to about $2,250. Putting it in perspective, I realized a 1560% return on my investment or 1460% profit. When was the last time you realized such a return on an investment of any kind? It is a very nice experience that you too can realize as soon as you get things going and gain a little experience.

A customer of my CD-ROM book barely had time to skim through my book before such a book sale kicked off in her town. She frantically asked me about lookup services so that she could use her cell phone to look books up at the sale, but when she got to the sale, she found it was in a warehouse with almost no cell phone reception. I was very happy to hear that she curtailed her enthusiasm and only bought the books she was able to look up and confirm to be winners. Too often, people get into online bookselling and attend a large library book sale before they know what they are doing, and almost every one of them has filled a bunch of bookshelves with firewood. Don't let your enthusiasm overwhelm your good sense or patience. As you buy and sell books that you know are good, you will develop an experience based sense for what is good and what is firewood. Then, when you do attend a library book sale and buy books without looking them up, the number of winners will far outnumber the ones of firewood value. I just don't want you to go out and waste your money on firewood and become discouraged. Buying books for your inventory with no experience and no tools to help determine their values is analogous to sitting down at a poker table in Las Vegas and playing without knowing any of the rules of the game.

A good resource for finding library book sales is through a subscription notification at BookSaleFinder.com.

## BookSaleFinder.com

BookSaleFinder.com is not only a place to find some good books; it is a great resource for locating the upcoming book sales in your area. You can even sign up to receive free email notification each week of those sales.

On the BookSaleFinder.com website there are a number of classified advertisements that list buyers and sellers of books. While I have never bought any books through the BookSaleFinder.com classified, I have purchased books listed on the banner advertisements.

A while back there was a seller that had thousands of books listed that he had purchased from a government library that had closed and consolidated with other libraries in the system. I purchased a number of valuable books from him, and while I have not recovered my investment yet, I did not expect to for quite some time as these books are specialized engineering books.

Anyway, I would highly recommend not only checking out BookSaleFinder.com, but that you sign up for book sale notifications.

The staff at BookSaleFinder.com is very friendly, helpful, and knowledgeable, so they are constantly looking for ways to enhance their service and are being noticed by more and more sales events. Consequently, the value of their website and the book sale information posted on it is getting better all the time.

## Consignment

This is a difficult subject to address for multiple reasons. It can be a very lucrative and synergistic arrangement, but you could also end up storing a bunch of worthless books for others.

If and when you choose to enter into a consignment agreement, you are accepting the property of someone else and agreeing to sell it for him or her in return for a sales commission. You are responsible for their property while it is in your possession and this could require that you carry additional insurance to cover that property. You also need to have a legal agreement – in writing – with them that declares everything about the arrangement, i.e., exactly what property you are accepting on consignment, what you are charging for a sales commission, how long you will retain the property for the purpose of selling it, what becomes of the property if it does not sell, etc.

If you are thinking of selling books on a consignment basis, I would strongly encourage you to pay a visit to an attorney and have him/her write a consignment contract for you to use that is specifically tailored to suit your needs.

The upside to selling on a consignment basis is that you will quite likely get a lot more books in your inventory to sell at no cost to you.

Another consideration you might ponder before accepting books on a consignment basis is to let your potential consignment customers know that you are not willing to accept just any book they might want to sell, possibly by putting a minimum selling price value on any book you are willing to take.

As I stated before, I do accept books from an estate liquidator on a consignment basis, but I go through the estate and identify the books that I feel are worth bothering with. If I just took every book being sold at the estate and let the liquidator purchase it from the estate for a dollar, his return on his investment might be too little to bother calling me again, or it could even be negative. For this reason I am very selective about the books I choose and let him purchase.

## Classified Advertisement

There is nothing wrong with running your own classified advertisement stating that you will buy used books and/or collections directly from the public. You might also consider running such an advertisement stating that you will donate a percentage of proceeds to a charity if the readers of the advertisement will donate their books to you for resale.

Bear in mind that if you run such an advertisement and tell people you will pay cash for their books, you are going to get a response and you need to have a consistent response to some of the questions you are going to be asked, e.g., are you going to buy anything that is offered, or are you going to be selective about what you buy? You are likely to get many responses to your ad, but the majority will be to sell you their books that are worth almost nothing and you need to have your story straight before you get inundated with calls. Of course, you may very well get some outstanding books for your inventory too, but choose your advertisement wording carefully, you don't want everyone reading the New York Times to think you are out to buy anything that is offered.

## Bulletin Board Index Card

If you live in a community where people are allowed to advertise their businesses on bulletin boards using index cards, you might consider something like the following:

---

GET $$$ CASH $$$ FOR YOUR BOOKS

HELP YOUR FAVORITE SCHOOL, LIBRARY, OR COMMUNITY FUNDRAISING EFFORT

[Your bookstore name], is a locally owned and operated bookseller with hundreds of millions of potential customers, and [Your bookstore name] will make a $$$ CASH $$$ donation of [a percentage you decide]% to the school, library, community fundraising effort, or club of your choice, based on the sales price of the books you donate.

Books must be in very good condition.

Contact us at: [Your phone number]
For more information or to schedule a donation

---

I want to warn you, because I have run such a bulletin board advertisement, that you better be prepared, you will be getting calls. You need to decide before you run such an ad:

1) What types of books you will accept.

2) What will become of the books that do not sell

3) If you are going to accept all the books that are donated

4) If you are going to allow donations to any charity or if you will provide the donors with a list of those charities you are prepared to let them select from.

5) What the tax implications of the donation are, i.e., will you be taking the tax deduction or will you allow the donors to take the deduction.

6) How you are going to let the donors know what donation is being made on their behalf.

7) Do you want to use your home phone number for inquiries?

8) How soon will you be listing the donated books for sale and how frequently will you report the sales and associated charity donations to the book donors?

9) Are you going to question the donors on the phone to determine if the books they want to donate are books you will accept.

10) What do you intend to do with books that do not sell and how long will you continue to list them?

11) What are you going to tell a customer that suggests that the donations should be to him/her? This is a consignment scenario, so you need to have an answer.

This type of an arrangement is something of a consignment arrangement and you need to establish these things up front – before you run such an advertisement.

Another benefit to this type of offering is that if you make the donations directly to the charitable organizations, you may very well establish an ongoing relationship with them and they may contact you to sell larger lots of books for them on a consignment basis. I have tried to establish just such a relationship with my local library, but owing to the charity nature of their *Friends of the Library* organization, they were unable to do this.

## University Professors

If you live near a university, it might be worth your time and effort to visit with a few professors. Many times when a professor moves from one university to another, or when they retire, they put large stacks of books in the hallways outside their offices for anyone to take. They also put many books out at the end of a semester that were left in their classrooms during the year. If you can strike up a relationship with a few of these professors, they may just give you a phone call when they want to clean out their offices, or when they know another professor is going to be doing so. This is a long shot, but I know it works because my son has been able to pick up hundreds of college textbooks doing it. You might also consider just wandering the halls of the university to gather books that are left out at the end of a semester. Some schools will put these books in the engineering library or the general library for anyone that wants them to take.

# How Much To Pay For Books

If you go to the same type of places that I go to buy your inventory, i.e., library book sales, thrift shops, and estate sales, you will find that almost all books sell for $3 or less. Sometimes the library shelves where I go will have some computer related books for as much as $20, and I will not pass them up if I can make $20 on them, but I do look them up before I buy them because I have found that the people that do the book pricing at my library do not have any idea of a book's value when they assign a price. For example, I picked up the three-volume set of Lives of the Puritans the other day for $3. This three volume set sells for $285 on Amazon.com. The same day I found a book on Java applications selling for $5 that sells on Amazon.com for $0.01.

Do you remember that book I told you about that I bought for $0.25 and sold to the United Nations for $260.04? That was a very good example of a nice price to pay for a book to sell, but it is not the best example. This week, I was in California attending a job related conference and while I was gone, my stepdaughter bought a book for $1.00 at my local library that sells for $2,250.00!!! That is the best buy I have ever experienced, and while it might take a year to sell, the Amazon.com rank is good enough that I am sure it will sell for this much. This sounds great, but I will tell you that such finds are rare and you should not expect to run into one like this very often.

The *Friends of the Library* shelves usually have the best buys for books to supply your inventory, but Estate Sales are not far behind, nor are thrift stores, both of which usually have some gems that only sell for a few dollars more.

I guess the central theme I am trying to convey is that it does not really matter too much to me how much I pay for a book, I am more interested in whether I can sell it for a profit in a reasonable period of time. I am quite happy to pay $50 for a book if I can turn around and sell it for a $40 profit in a few days.

I have heard other online booksellers say they won't buy a book unless it will turn a $10 profit. I think that is a great philosophy if you can find enough of these books, but I have no problem buying a book for a dollar if I can make two dollars. The subscription fees and lookup services get paid off quickly by these lower profit books and the gems return the larger profits that ultimately make it all worthwhile. For books that are priced under $5 I do try to make sure they will turn at least a couple dollars profit, but I think you also have to keep things in perspective. A 300% profit on a $1 book is pretty good, and that same 300% profit will buy you a few soft drinks that would have to come out of your pocket if you hadn't turned the profit – or, it will buy a few more books, one of which might be a gem that makes you a few hundred dollars.

# What Books To Buy And Which To Avoid

This certainly sounds like it is easy enough, and while I don't want to discourage you or make it sound unreasonably difficult, I don't want you to think it is trivial.

Up front I want you to forget about the novels and mystery books you like, and eliminate any notion that you might have that the more popular a title, the more likely it is to sell, because while this is true, the selling price of most popular books is about a penny. In fact, if a title is very popular there were probably hundreds of thousands of copies printed, and the value to you as a seller of used books is probably nil. I have found very few popular books of any value, and if they did have a resale value it was probably because they were autographed by the author. At the same time, new books that just came out and have not saturated the market can generally turn a few dollars profit. One exception I will make is books that are being made into movies. Many times, even though the market was previously saturated, the demand for a book will quickly pick up as soon as the public learns that a movie is being made from the story of a book.

I will not usually bother looking up new novels or mystery books unless I cannot identify others that I recognize as more likely to make money, i.e., if I run out of books I feel are good prospects and still have some time on my hands, I will look up some of these others, but this is not too often and the time is better spent on books I know are likely to turn a profit.

If you think you can walk into a book sale, garage sale, library sale, or used book store clearance sale and buy books for your inventory without any tools at your disposal, I wish you luck and suspect you will fill your book shelves with firewood. You may be able to get away with this at a big library book sale out of necessity to decide quickly in the bookseller buying frenzy, but I suggest you get some buying experience under your belt first.

You need to know the value of a book **BEFORE** you buy it. With the Internet at your disposal, there are a couple ways you can find out what the value of a book is before you pay anything for it, and you can even determine the sales ranking for most. Both methods I use involve a cell phone.

The "poor man's" beginning point is to have someone at home look books up for you while you tell them the ISBN over a cell phone. When I first started this is what I would do, I would call my wife at home when I was out buying books from my cell phone and have her look up books for me on the Internet and tell me the used prices so I could determine if a book was worth purchasing. If my wife was not available to help, I used my unlimited Internet access on my cell phone to look them up, but accessing the Internet and doing the research through a cell phone can be much slower if you do not sign up for a book value research tool.

The most efficient way to look up books is on the Internet through a cell phone and a subscription look-up tool. My favorite is ASellerTool.com. For $4.99 per month I have access to their website and in just a couple seconds I can get the three lowest prices for a book through Amazon.com, the new price through Amazon.com, the title of the book, and the Amazon.com sales rank, the number of used copies for sale on Amazon.com, and the number of new copies for sale on Amazon.com, just by entering the book's ISBN number. Let me explain the value of this information to me:

1) The three lowest Amazon.com sales prices are useful because if all I asked for was the lowest, it might be for a book in deplorable shape or a lowball seller. If I see that there is a big gap between the lowest and the next lowest, this is exactly what I will assume. For example, if the three lowest prices displayed were: $2.35 $12.65, and $12.69, I would assume the one being offered on Amazon.com for $2.35 was an exceptionally poor copy that someone just wants to unload, or a book being sold by a lowball seller that does not have a clue as to its worth.

2) The new price that the book is selling on Amazon.com for is useful because in many cases the book I am buying is indeed a new book and there can be quite a difference between the value of a new book and a used book. There are also times when the new price is substantially lower than the used book price. There could be a couple reasons for this:

   a. Someone has bought a large number of books with this title from a wholesale or remainder distributor and has undercut the used book prices to sell their new remainder copies.
   b. Amazon.com has picked up this title and started selling it new after a bunch of online booksellers listed used copies, and the online booksellers have not checked to see that their prices are competitive.

   Regardless, it is important to know both the new and used price of a title in order to make a determination of the resale value.

3) The title is a check I use for myself. Since I enter only the ISBN number for the book I am inquiring about, if I don't ask for the title to be displayed I run the risk of getting information for a book other than the one I really want to know about. If I am looking up a book and I am told it is worth $25 I am going to buy it, but without checking that the title in the requested information matches the title of the book I am looking up, I cannot be sure the returned information is for the book I want to know about. It is very easy to type the wrong ISBN number into my cell phone.

4) The Amazon.com sales rank gives me an indication of how quickly the book might sell, i.e., the popularity or demand for the book. Books with very low ranks, 1 to 100,000 tend to sell within a week, those between 100,000 and 1,000,000 can take a month to eighteen months, and those with ranks of 1,000,000 to 3,000,000 can take a long time to sell. These are just guidelines I have found from my own experiences, and how quickly a book with any rank might sell is certainly influenced by the asking price and condition as well.

There is one scenario where getting books for your inventory warrants blind buying, but I would not suggest participating until you have a better idea of what books have a resale value to you. Library book sales are heavily populated with other booksellers doing the same thing as you are considering doing. This is especially true of the pre-sale events offered by most library book sales where they charge admission the day before the sale opens to the public. Book dealers attend these pre-sale events because they get the opportunity to buy books for their inventory before the sale opens to the public. These events can be quite hectic as there are many dealers attending and they are grabbing up books as fast as they perceive a resale value.

When I attend these events I typically take my wife and pay double admission because she helps by taking the boxes I have filled with books to a neutral location and watches over them to make sure other dealers do not start taking the books I intend to buy.

I have also observed many dealers hoarding books. This is the act of grabbing up large numbers of books, moving them to a neutral location and then looking them up to determine their value before buying them. I consider these dealers amateurs, but it is annoying and many of these events are recognizing this behavior and banning it. I know my son deals with this in his used book selling business too. He told me that he attended a university book sale and took my other son along to help. He said there were dozens of other dealers there with cell phones hoarding them and trying to look them up before buying them. While they were waiting for their cell phones to give them answers, he loaded his shopping carts with other books right in front of them, and based on his experience at determining book values, he loaded seven shopping carts with books that he did buy. He ended up with over 600 books and only about a dozen turned out being firewood. He paid less than a dollar each for the books he bought and within 72 hours one of the books sold for over $750.

I am not suggesting you should go to a library sale and buy whatever you can get your hands on, in fact, I suggest exactly the opposite, i.e., don't even go until you have at least some experience at establishing values without looking them up. I don't know books well enough to identify winners like my son, and I have been doing this for almost five years. I wouldn't even go to an event like this until I had been doing this business for a couple years and had looked up thousands of books. If you try doing it without experience, I can almost assure you that you will lose money on the ordeal and will buy a lot of firewood. Besides having to pay for the books you buy at such an event, you will have to pay an admission, which is usually $25 per person.

Now, equally important as knowing how to research book values is to know which books to bother looking up. It is very difficult to tell you in general terms that any kind of book is good, but there are types of books that usually have more potential than others. College textbooks are generally worth looking up, as are any books having the yellow "USED" stickers on the spine as this is usually a college text as well. Also, science, medicine, engineering, physics, and legal reference books are usually worth looking up. There are also a number of activity books for children and many are worth researching. You will find a number of books in self-help, religion, and do-it-yourself sections that are worth looking up, but you will also find a lot of firewood in these sections. You will just have to get the experience by looking them up and learning which are firewood and which are worth buying. The only general advice I can really give is to seek unusual books that are normally published in small quantities. There are many cases that I can remember when a book sells for ten times the original cover price simply because the original was published in a small quantity and the book is no longer in publication. Every year thousands of books go out of publication, these are the gems of our future, and if you pick up a book that says "Over A Million Copies Sold" on the front cover, you can be reasonably certain it is on Amazon.com for pennies.

It is generally much easier to put particular classes of books in the firewood category than to identify winner categories. I generally do not waste any time looking up novels, financial books intended to teach people about the stock market, psychology books (even the college texts), auto maintenance manuals, biographies, or cookbooks. There are a few exceptions to these rules, but the time spent looking through the massive quantities of these books is usually not worth spending and I prefer concentrating on others with more winners.

In my experience, researching book values is a lot like playing slot machines. You type in the ISBN number and pull the lever to see if it is a winner. The only big difference I see between the two is that you do not lose anything if the book turns out to be firewood; you just have to type in another ISBN number and try again. The only time the analogy results in you losing as in the slot machine scenario is when you purchase the books before looking them up. If you do your research correctly, you will seldom lose unless you pick books that are not in demand or the market gets flooded with similar copies after you put yours up for sale.

When you are doing your price research to enter new inventory, I recommend Chambal.com. By entering ISBN numbers or title and author on their website, you will be given the current price for similar books on all the major websites. Other resources I use are Amazon.com's advanced lookup, Half.com, BarnesandNoble.com, and BookFinder.com. In Appendix B, I have put links to each of these price lookup sites. For many books you can also find a ranking on the Amazon.com website that is indicative of the demand for that book. The lower the Amazon.com ranking number, the higher the demand. i.e., the Amazon.com ranking is a sales rank or bestseller's list if you will. A ranking below 500,000 will generally sell within two months if you price it competitively. The Amazon.com sales rank can also be displayed on your cell phone using the ASellerTool.com software subscription. To give you an idea of the selling time associated with the Amazon.com sales rank, I have included a couple charts below that reflect my experience with the books I have bought and sold.

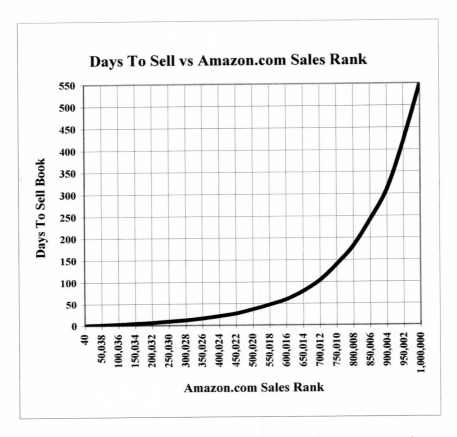

This chart demonstrates the non-linear relationship between the Amazon.com sales rank and the average time I have found a book with a corresponding rank to sell. For a book with an Amazon.com sales rank in excess of 1,000,000, I have found it to take an average time of over a year to sell. This does not mean that it always takes a year to sell a book with an Amazon.com sales rank this high, but since I do not price my books at the lowest price available, this is what I have experienced on average. I will also tell you that I have had a book with an Amazon.com sales rank in excess of 2,000,000 sell in less than a month. Apparently the buyer was looking for one in better condition than the lowest priced copy available and decided to buy mine.

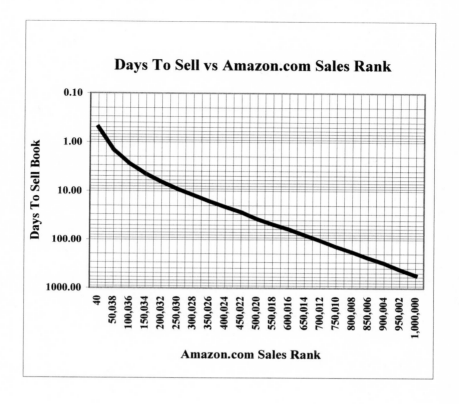

I also wanted to show that a semi-logarithmic plot of the same data is very nearly linear for Amazon.com sales ranks from approximately 100,000 to 1,000,000. This may not be of interest to you, but as an engineer I found it curious because it suggests a relationship between the days it takes to sell a book and the Amazon.com sales rank of the form:

$$y = bm^x$$

where,

y = Amazon.com sales rank
b = y intercept
m = Slope
x = The number of days it takes to sell a book

Solving for x gives us:

$$x = \ln(y/b) / \ln(m)$$

Having solved for the slope and intercept values for my own data, I have found the equation to fit my data with a correlation coefficient of 0.93 which suggests a very good fit to the data.

I do not want to turn this into a mathematical dissertation; I only wanted to demonstrate that there is a very good correlation between the Amazon.com sales rank and the number of days I have found it to take in selling a book with that sales rank.

I have also found this to compare quite well with other published information I have found on a few websites. Of course they have a slightly different slope and y intercept value in their data. The difference I am sure is attributable to differing pricing strategies and if you tend to price higher or lower than I do, chances are you will experience a different selling time period than I.

If there were a single slope and intercept value that applied to all booksellers, then you would know exactly when any given book would sell, but of course this is not going to happen because there are far too many variables of influence.

If you are not using a wireless lookup service and want to see the Amazon sales rank for any given book, just look the book up on the Amazon.com website and then look at the "Product Details" for the book. You will see two Amazon sales ranks given, the current sales rank and yesterday's sales rank. Keep in mind that these are a measure of the sales trend for this book on Amazon only. If the book is a Barnes and Noble publication, it might be selling like crazy through Barnes and Noble and selling very few copies on Amazon. My own book seems to sell better through direct purchase using PayPal than through the Amazon website, thus I do not maintain a very low Amazon sales rank, but I do sell many books.

## Book-Of-The-Month Editions

I don't want to tell you that there are no book-of-the-month editions worth buying, but of the hundreds I have looked at over the past five years I have not found any worth purchasing. In fact, I gave up on them over four years ago because of this.

## Advance Uncorrected Proofs

Advance Uncorrected Proofs, sometimes labeled Uncorrected Reading Copy editions are generally worth checking out. There are some collectors out there that scoop these books up, so I do spend the time to research them. Sometimes you will find an Advance Uncorrected Proof and be able to market it before the first edition is even released. These tend to sell very quickly as there are readers that follow particular authors and they like to read a book before anyone else gets the opportunity. Many times an Advance Uncorrected Proof in paperback will sell for $20 and the first edition release in paperback will only sell for $6.99 new. So when you are browsing the shelves for inventory, keep your eye out for them, they will be clearly marked on the cover.

Of course, selling uncorrected proofs is a contradiction to everything the large publishers profess, they would like these copies to be destroyed when the review is complete. Fortunately, many reviewers still donate these books to libraries or sell them to brick and mortar storefronts where as an online bookseller I quite frequently buy them for a buck and sell them for ten.

## E-books

E-books are electronic books. They are sometimes books on a CD, or just files that are emailed. You can buy collections of e-books with resale rights, but not many are very good for resale or the people selling them to you would not offer resale rights, they would sell them to the consumers themselves and keep the profits, after all, all you have to do with them per the advertisements is to email them after collecting the money from the sale. Do you really think they would be selling something this easy to deliver if there was a profit to be made?

You can get e-books for free to market yourself. There are a number of Internet sources where you can get a free copy of a book that is no longer copyright protected. You can clean these files up and create electronic copies that you too can sell. It is both legal and ethical, but a few of the online marketplaces do not allow the marketing of any work for which you do not have publishing rights. This should include e-books of works that have expired copyrights, but for some reason some of the online marketplaces do not want to allow it; perhaps it is just a line of risk they do not wish to approach.

You can also write your own books and market them. If there is something you know well that you think there is a market for, by all means write a book about it and see if there is a demand for the information. You can even register your book and get an ISBN number for it that will make it easier for buyers to find and marketplaces to list, but to get an ISBN you must offer the book in tangible form, an e-book will qualify for an ISBN by itself, but you should burn CD's and ship them.

I know an individual that is a fanatic about the Ford Mustang. He wrote a very short book about the rebuilding of a Mustang engine and has done pretty well marketing it on eBay.com. While I have never asked him the specifics of his success, the tracking of his auctions and bids received would indicate sales of at least 100 copies at around $30 a copy. The book he wrote is only about 40 pages and is mostly captioned photographs; it couldn't have taken him more than a weekend to put together.

To me, one of the greatest drawbacks to e-books is the protection of intellectual property. It should suffice to copyright a work, but piracy is prolific and e-books are easy to copy and distribute, for this reason alone the added step of ISBN registration and copyright filing should be done.

Even this book is a good example. I know there are other authors out there that have written similar books, I have even read parts of their books, but I felt I could put together a comprehensive book on the subject that would include a lot of information I felt was omitted from other works. I also felt there was a lot more value in the practical operations end of the business than in telling you how to structure the legal end of your business while at the same time telling you I am not a lawyer and cannot give legal advice. Finally, I felt that if you want to get in the online bookselling business, you would get more value out of a book that comes on CD and has all the hyperlinks you will need as your business grows, but alas, my customers have convinced me that despite the efficiency loss, they would prefer my book in paperback. Who wants to try and find something in a paperback by going through every page to find what they are looking for when they can do a document search to find the topic and then click on a hyperlink? Apparently, a majority of my customers and potential customers do prefer a paperback.

# How To Price And Grade Your Books

## Determining What You Have

Before you start trying to price and grade your books, you need to know what they are, i.e., when they were published, what edition they are, etc. So, lets begin by first determining the year of the publication.

Many older books and some newer ones still, use Roman Numerals to date the publication. Yeah, it is easy to read the date if it is written in numbers we all know, but how are we going to decipher when it was published if the date is given in Roman Numerals?

I have included a couple tables here to help you with dates given in Roman Numerals.

## Table Of Roman Numerals

| Centuries In Roman Numerals | | | |
|---|---|---|---|
| 1000 | M | 1600 | MDC |
| 1100 | MC | 1700 | MDCC |
| 1200 | MCC | 1800 | MDCCC |
| 1300 | MCCC | 1900 | MCM |
| 1400 | MCD | 2000 | MM |
| 1500 | MD | 2100 | MMC |

| Years In Roman Numerals | | | | | | | |
|---|---|---|---|---|---|---|---|
| 1 | I | 26 | XXVI | 51 | LI | 76 | LXXVI |
| 2 | II | 27 | XXVII | 52 | LII | 77 | LXXVII |
| 3 | III | 28 | XXVIII | 53 | LIII | 78 | LXXVIII |
| 4 | IV | 29 | XXIX | 54 | LIV | 79 | LXXIX |
| 5 | V | 30 | XXX | 55 | LV | 80 | LXXX |
| 6 | VI | 31 | XXXI | 56 | LVI | 81 | LXXXI |
| 7 | VII | 32 | XXXII | 57 | LVII | 82 | LXXXII |
| 8 | VIII | 33 | XXXIII | 58 | LVIII | 83 | LXXXIII |
| 9 | IX | 34 | XXXIV | 59 | LIX | 84 | LXXXIV |
| 10 | X | 35 | XXXV | 60 | LX | 85 | LXXXV |
| 11 | XI | 36 | XXXVI | 61 | LXI | 86 | LXXXVI |
| 12 | XII | 37 | XXXVII | 62 | LXII | 87 | LXXXVII |
| 13 | XIII | 38 | XXXVIII | 63 | LXIII | 88 | LXXXVIII |
| 14 | XIV | 39 | XXXIX | 64 | LXIV | 89 | LXXXIX |
| 15 | XV | 40 | XL | 65 | LXV | 90 | XC |
| 16 | XVI | 41 | XLI | 66 | LXVI | 91 | XCI |
| 17 | XVII | 42 | XLII | 67 | LXVII | 92 | XCII |
| 18 | XVIII | 43 | XLIII | 68 | LXVIII | 93 | XCIII |
| 19 | XIX | 44 | XLIV | 69 | LXIX | 94 | XCIV |
| 20 | XX | 45 | XLV | 70 | LXX | 95 | XCV |
| 21 | XXI | 46 | XLVI | 71 | LXXI | 96 | XCVI |
| 22 | XXII | 47 | XLVII | 72 | LXXII | 97 | XCVII |
| 23 | XXIII | 48 | XLVIII | 73 | LXXIII | 98 | XCVIII |
| 24 | XXIV | 49 | XLIX | 74 | LXXIV | 99 | XCIX |
| 25 | XXV | 50 | L | 75 | LXXV | 100 | C |

The rules for Roman Numerals are really easy if you know the base units and the significance of their order.

The base units are:

I = 1
V = 5
X = 10
L = 50
C = 100
D = 500
M = 1000

All numbers are positive if they are to the right of larger units and negative if they are to the left of larger units.

Lets go through a couple examples:

Example 1

A book's date is given as: MCMLXXII

I try to decipher the dates a little differently than the conventional way of reading Roman Numerals. First I determine the century of the publication by matching the first few letters on the left with the values in the table for centuries.

M = 1000
C = -100 (Since it is to the left of a bigger number, the $2^{nd}$ M)
M = 1000

Thus, the century is:

1000 − 100 + 1000 = 1900

Then I decipher the last digits:

L = 50
X = 10
X = 10
II = 2

Thus, LXXII = 50 + 10 + 10 + 2 = 72

Now I know the date is: 1900 + 72 = 1972

Example 2

The book's given date is: MCDXCIX

Again, I determine the century:

M = 1000
C = -100 (Since it is to the left of a bigger number, the D)
D = 500

Thus, the century is:

1000 − 100 + 500 = 1400

At this point, I really wouldn't care about the rest of the date and I would buy the book if I could afford it, but to complete the example I will go through the rest of the date determination.

Next, the year:

X = -10 (Since it is to the left of a bigger number, C)
C = 100
I = -1 (Since it is to the left of a bigger number, X)
X = 10

Thus, the year is:

-10 + 100 − 1 + 10 = 99

The year of the publication is: 1400 + 99 = 1499

If you learn the base units and play with the numbers for a little while I am sure you will get the hang of it. Besides, you will probably find books that have dates beginning with MM (2000), MCM (1900) and perhaps a few that start with MDCCC (1800). You really only need to know these and how to decipher the decade and year to add to these numbers.

One of the next things you want to determine about a book is the edition and date of it.

## Edition

Sometimes determining the edition is not as simple as it sounds, and sometimes a book that has "First Edition" printed in it is not really a first edition, but is a first edition by the publisher that printed it. Sometimes a book states it is a first edition, but it is a first edition by that particular book of the month club. While this may not seem particularly interesting to you, it generally always means a substantial difference in the value of the book.

In most cases, with the exception of book of the month club first editions, the books you run across in the shelves of the *Friends of the Library*, in thrift stores, at garage sales, and at library book sales will be first editions if they state first edition, but be wary of those book of the month editions.

Books that state they are a "First Edition" and say nothing more, are usually also a first printing, but you need to determine if this is true by deciphering whether it is a first printing or not.

Look for a string of numbers from one to ten. They are not always printed in order, but if there is a one present and the book says it is a "First Edition," then it is also a first printing. There is one exception to this that I am aware of, the publisher Random House will use a two and state "First Edition" for a "First Edition," first printing.

There are books that will show number strings much higher than one through ten, e.g.,

54   55 56 57 58 59 60 61 62 63

If you find a book like this, it is usually a waste of time to bother looking it up, it is the 54th printing of this edition and the market is probably swamped with copies of this book.

Another subtle way that publishers have for letting you know that the copy you are looking at is not a "First Edition" is the use of a phrase like:

First published 1959

or by comparing the copyright date with the printing date. If these two dates are not the same, you probably do not have a "First Edition" of any sort.

In the last two decades, the number of collectors that are looking for "First Edition," first print copies, has really escalated and finding these editions to sell has become the mainstay for many booksellers. If you want to focus on providing these copies to collectors and have the patience to identify them, you might just have a niche that will make you some good money. I run across these copies on occasion by accident, but I do not seek them out.

## What Is In The ISBN

A large number of the books you will find have an ISBN with an EAN barcode, but there are still a lot of books out there that do not have a barcode at all. In this case, you will not find any information in the ISBN except the number itself. In some older books, you will find an SSN and with many of these you can add a leading zero and have the ISBN. This does not always hold true, but if it works, it makes looking the book up with a wireless lookup service a lot easier than typing the title and author. Some books have both the 10 digit ISBN and the 13 digit ISBN. Over the next couple years, all books will be assigned a 13 digit ISBN because the number of titles is approaching the number of available and unique 10 digit combinations. Right now the books with a 13 digit ISBN have a 978 as their first three numbers, the remaining 10 are usually the same as the 10 digit ISBN. You might find the look a little confusing, as they will be listed something like the example below.

ISBN-13: 978-1-59971-487-6
ISBN-10: 1-59971-487-6

These are the 13 and 10 digit ISBN's assigned to the CD-ROM version of my book.

There is a bit more to the ISBN/EAN barcode than just a number. For example, the publisher's list price is a part of the ISBN barcode as well as the currency and language of the book. I don't want to get too far into the details, but I do want to at least touch on the more common parts that you will encounter on a regular basis and show you by the example below what you might expect to decipher from the books you will look at regularly.

Last four digits are book price code, here the book is $39.99, the first number is a currency code, 5 means dollars, a 0 would mean UK pounds

The book ISBN

ISBN 1-59971-487-6

53999

9 781599 714875

The 13 digit ISBN EAN barcode, begins with 978, and all other numbers are the same as previous 10 digit ISBN except last check digit. Eventually, the 978 will be replaced by 979.

This is the ISBN and EAN barcode taken from my CD-ROM book. The first thing I want to point out is that from this, you can determine that the original publisher's price for the book is 39.99, and since the 3999 is preceded by a 5, the units of currency are dollars. A book with 03999 would be £39.99, or 39.99 British Pounds. There are other codes for other currencies, but a "0" or "5" are the most common codes you will encounter. It is also worth noting that a book with code of 50000 has a publisher's list price exceeding $99.99, or the price was not established by the time the ISBN was assigned, and a book with five zeros was similarly in excess of £99.99 or did not have a price established when the ISBN was assigned. If you pick up books with a 50000 or 00000 code, they are usually worth taking a good look at.

There really isn't much more to the barcode than that, but these little tips can make your job of finding worthwhile books a lot easier and faster if you are trying to identify some high dollar books at a book sale. They can also save you a lot of time by not bothering with the ones with small numbers like 50299, because, unless they are rare, they probably won't be worth much.

## Pricing Tools

Before you price your books it is a good idea to have an educated understanding of what other's have priced the same book for AND the condition of the copies they have listed.

As I told you before, I use ASellerTool.com to get the Amazon.com price for books when I am buying, but when I get the books home and start the listing and pricing of them I use another Internet tool which is free. Personally I prefer Chambal.com because it returns the prices for books listed on a number of marketplaces, including:

Half.com
Amazon.com
Alibris.com
Abebooks.com
A1books.com
Biblio.com
Powells.com
Walmart.com
Buy.com
Overstock.com
Textbookx.com
Ecampus.com
BarnesandNoble.com
Blackwell.com
ebay.com

I have found that researching book prices using Chambal.com takes a little longer, but it is a very thorough tool and returns not only used book prices, but also new and third party new prices. The search results also return links to other copies being marketed so I can investigate further if I desire.

Using the information I get from a Chambal.com search, and the condition of the book I have, I establish a price to market my copy. I will delve into my pricing logic later in this chapter, but I want you to understand that the price I establish for books I sell is not just tied to the going prices of other copies, condition, demand, whether or not it is a first edition, and such things as author autographs also play into my pricing. Sometimes I even price a book a little higher just because I would prefer to keep it for myself if I cannot get a little more for it.

If the book I am trying to price does not have an ISBN number, Chambal.com allows me to search by title and author as well. If no pricing information is returned by a Chambal.com search, I will often use BookFinder.com. When the Bookfinder.com website initially comes up, there does not appear to be a field to enter an ISBN number, but it can be entered in the title field and their website is intelligent enough to recognize it.

There are a number of other available pricing tools available on the Internet. Amazon.com has a very useful one, and in most cases I will use the Chambal.com price returned for books being sold on Amazon.com because about 65% of the books I sell online are sold through Amazon.com. When I do use the Amazon.com book-pricing tool, I generally use the advanced option to get more thorough information. Half.com, and BarnesandNoble.com websites also have pricing tools.

## Book Condition And Grading

There are a number of resources and standards for grading books, the Independent Online Booksellers Association, IOBA, is a good reference, and they can be accessed simply at: http://www.ioba.org.

They give a finer resolution grading scale that has more grades than I generally use or that are available for the online marketplaces.

When you are assigning grades to your books, be conservative. Your customers will appreciate getting a book in better condition that it was described, and they will certainly leave you negative feedback – or return the book – if it arrives in worse condition than you described it.

The grades I use are:

## New

This is a book that is truly new. One without any defects and is in immaculate condition. Generally, I will only list a book as new if it IS new. If a book looks new, but it has been opened and read, it will not qualify as new.

## As New

I will grade a book As New if it is in the same shape as a new book, but has been read. If I list a book As New, it cannot have soiled pages, dog-eared pages, a damaged dust jacket or cover, or any other visible flaws. I tend to think of As New books as being a book that someone bought, thumbed through, never fully opened to read, and kept in a safe place where no damage was done to the cover or dust jacket. Many times I will list a flawless book with minor dust jacket gloss scuffing As New, but I will also state in the listing that the dust jacket has minor gloss scuffing owing to shelving, adjacent books, or use. Don't try to pass off a book that is Very Good for a book that is As New.

## Very Good

This is a used book with minor defects, small signs of wear, or other minor imperfections. If a book is very clean and crisp, and has a few - and I do mean only a few sentences that are highlighted or underlined, I will sometimes list it as Very Good, but I will also note that there is minor highlighting or underlining in my listing.

## Good

A book that is listed as Good has obvious signs of use, e.g., worn covers, dinged or bent corners on a hardback, some highlighting or underlining, and would generally be considered to be in average shape. The binding should still be solid and all pages should be intact.

## Acceptable

This would be a book with solid binding and a lot of obvious use, e.g., lots of highlighting, underlining, and or notes written throughout. It is a book that is not pretty but is still fully functional.

## Listing Notes

When listing your books, be honest. Do not try to sneak a book into the Very Good category if it is only Good. Also include things such as a previous owner's name written on the first blank or inside the cover, gift inscriptions, any highlighting, underlining, margin notes, dog-eared pages, bumped, banged, or curled covers, water damage, yellowing of pages, torn pages, ex-library copy with library ownership markings, etc. I have found that if you describe a book accurately and someone buys it, they will not be disappointed when they get it. In fact, over the past several years I have only had one book out of the thousands I have sold get returned because the customer did not feel it was in as good of a condition as I had listed it. You should also not believe that a book would not sell just because it was in a poorer condition.

A few years ago I found a book about flying squirrels. It was a paperback and was in acceptable condition. The covers were heavily worn and the pages were tattered and a little foxing. I could not find a copy for sale anywhere else in the world, so I bought it for a quarter. A week later I sold the book for $29.99 and the customer paid another $22.00 to have it expedited to the United Kingdom. They were thrilled to get the book and very happy to pay the price I was asking. This is not an isolated incident, I am amazed weekly by some of the book sales I get for books that are not in very good condition, but I am honest about the conditions of my books listed and I note things as mentioned earlier.

There are also good and bad listing notes. Saying something like the book is As New, but it is a remainder and the publisher removed the front cover, this is not only a contradiction, it sounds stupid. Spend some time reading the book descriptions that others put on their listings and ask yourself which are good and which are deceiving. Strive to be honest and descriptive. I have listed many books that only get a grade of Very Good because they are new books that have some scuffing of the DJ's owing to sliding against adjacent books on the shelf. I may even tell the prospective customer that it is a new book and that it has a scuffed DJ in the book description, but I list the book as Very Good, not As New.

## Establishing A Price

Getting a general feel for the appropriate price for a book is not too difficult; it will be relatively straightforward from a price search through Chambal.com, Amazon.com, Half.com, BarnesandNoble.com, BookFinder.com, or one of the other online pricing tools.   What is a little more difficult is looking at all of this information and deciding on your asking price.

One of the best ways to put things in perspective with respect to book pricing is to keep in mind that none of your books have any value until they sell, and this is true of all products.  If you sell a book very quickly chances are you could have gotten more for it if you priced it a little higher and waited.  Similarly, if you price it too high the time it takes to sell it may be more influenced by economic inflationary trends than demand, i.e., if you price it high but it takes a hundred years to sell at that price, the fact that it finally sold at your high price probably has more to do with inflation and devaluation of currency than with a tangible value.  That is why I tend toward low-end prices, but not the lowest price.

## Setting A Lowest Price

By making the price of your book the lowest price available on the Internet you will almost certainly turn your inventory quickly, but you may unnecessarily minimize your profits as well and you will certainly not be very popular with the other online booksellers you have undercut.  This mentality has led to the demise of many online booksellers and made online bookselling very competitive.   There is probably nothing more detrimental to online book sales than other online booksellers that insist on low-ball pricing.   It only takes a few of these dealers with adequate inventory to drive a book's price down to nothing, and in doing so they only hurt themselves in the long run.  If you are going to undertake this business adventure, use some common sense, price and grade your books fairly and don't put yourself or others out of business by low-balling your prices.

If you do a search for popular mystery novels, works of fiction, and many other popular books, you will find most are available for a penny.  This is partly because the lowest price bookseller attitude has driven the price down as low as it can go and they are counting on recovering a few cents from their postage charges.

It is rare that I will set a book price as the lowest available and I would not suggest the practice to a new online seller either.

## Setting A Highest Price

Unless I have a very unusual or valuable rare book I will never opt for listing at the highest price, as it would result in very few sales.  If you run across a rare book that is autographed by the author and it has a very high collector value, you might opt for setting a price that is the highest for all available copies, otherwise do not practice setting the highest price or you are going to end up with a big personal collection.

## A Happy And Profitable Middle Ground

There is a middle ground with respect to book pricing that is profitable. As emphasized before, the grade of your book will play a substantial part in the book's pricing; try to fit your copy in with the price of others of comparable grades. You should also consider the demand for a particular book. Those in high demand will sell many copies a day from the assorted marketplaces and pricing too low will result in a quick sale that could possibly have been a bit more profitable if it were listed for a couple dollars more.

A lot of the art of pricing books to sell is just plain common sense if you at least know where to find out what others are selling for. You cannot realistically market a VW microbus as a Jaguar and it will not command the same price.

## Setting A Selling Price

After doing your pricing research and determining the going price for a particular book, an investigation that you should be able to complete within a minute for any given book, set a price that is comparable to the others you found. Don't set it as the lowest price available, but keep it among those near the lowest price of the same grade so it shows up on the first page of listings.

If your book does not sell within a reasonable period of time, say one month for a book that is in high demand and six months for an unusual and low demand book, you can always go back and update your listing price. In fact, it is a good idea to go back and review the pricing of any of your books that do not sell within the first six months of listing them to make sure they are still competitively priced to sell.

If you have a lot of books that do not sell it doesn't mean they are no good or not valuable, but they are no better than firewood if they never sell, so stay on top of them. At times, you will find a book or books in your inventory that seem to have dropped in price to almost nothing. These books are firewood and you should pull them from your inventory and donate them to a church, library, or thrift store. Keep a record of those you donate because it can be used as a tax deduction.

You also need to learn to forget what you paid for a book, i.e., if a book does not sell and you are adjusting prices when you learn that a particular book is now selling for less than you paid, price it to sell. Doing this will help to move the book and your losers will average out and be overwhelmed by your winners. Failing to price it competitively will only result in selling it for even less later when the price drops further, or donating it to some charity and taking a total loss on it because you were unwilling to price it competitively when you had the chance.

You will also need to find your own guidelines based on your limitations, e.g., how much space you have to store your inventory. These self-imposed guidelines will help you decide when is best to clear out your firewood. Do not be surprised if some of the older and more valuable titles you acquire take a couple years to sell.

I thought it might be useful here to give you some idea of a profit versus purchase price and a profit percentage versus purchase price distribution might look like. I have plotted about 3,200 book sales here to give you an idea.

In each of thee charts, the selling price and profit shown are exactly that, profit! I have already deducted the sales commissions, listing fees, packing materials, and other costs of doing business.

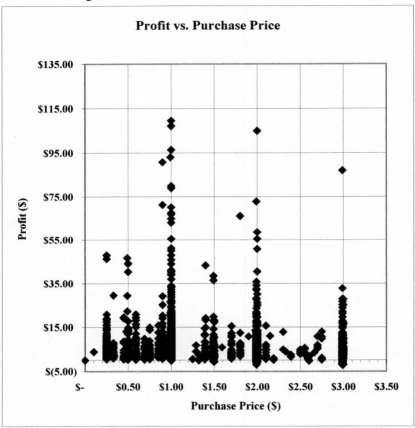

As you can see in this chart, the vast majority of books returned a profit of $35.00 or less, but 46 books did return profits in excess of $35.00, which equates to about 1.44%.

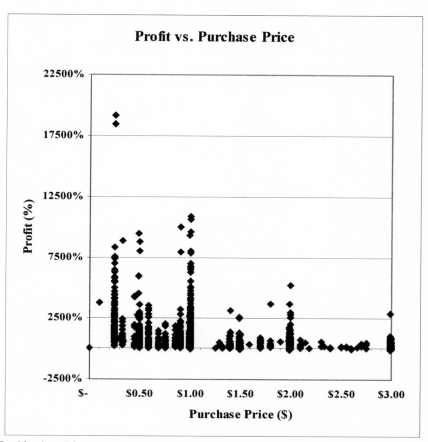

In this chart I have shown the percent profit versus purchase price. This is much more dramatic. Exactly 2,500 of the 3,200 book sales depicted in this graph returned a profit of 100% or more. In fact, it is useful to show a histogram of the profit percentages here as well.

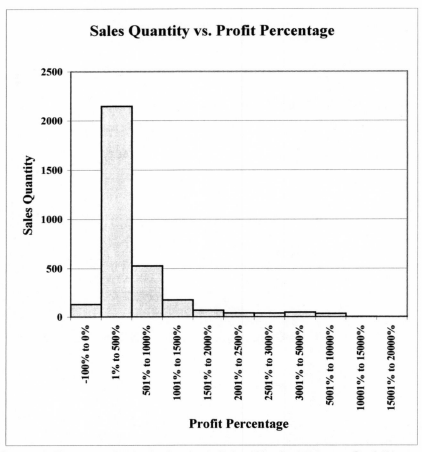

In this graph you can clearly see that the majority of books return a profit of 1% to 500%, with 1,561 returning 100% to 500%. That means getting back what was paid plus at least 100% profit for 1,561 of the 3,200 books sold. You can also see that more than 500 of the books included in this data paid for themselves and returned 501% to 1000% profit!

Does it sound attractive to buy a book for a dollar and sell it for $11.00? That is a 1000% profit. It even sounds better to buy one for $3.00 and sell it for $33.00.

The numbers alone do not mean a lot, but the dollars do, and when you have some data to compare, it would be very interesting to see if it follows similar trends. I just thought it might be useful here to show some data to give you a perspective on things that I have been unable to find in any other book on this topic.

The data represents a random block of sales that I extracted from my sales history. It is by no means indicative of what you will see, but it would not surprise me if you see similar trends.

## Examples Of Gems I Have Bought And Sold

I have included below a brief listing of some books I have made quite a bit of money selling, not to impress you, but to give you an idea of the unusual types of books to look for and the prices you can expect to get for unusual books.

*Real Estate Accounting and Mathematics Handbook/Book and Disk*, by Wiley, Robert J., Sold for $260.04, purchased for $0.25.

*Audio Cyclopedia*, by Tremaine, Howard M., Sold for $199.99, purchased for $1.00.

*Making Sense of Burgundy*, by Kramer, Matt, Sold for $125.75, purchased for $2.00.

*Wet Coastal Ecosystems*, by Chapman, Valentine J. (editor), Sold for $165.00, purchased for $0.49.

*Analysis And Design Of Airplane Structures*, by Bruhn, B.S., Sold for $129.75, purchased for $1.00.

*Color Science: Concepts and Methods, Quantitative Data and Formula*, by Wyszecki, Gunter; Stiles, W. S.; Wyszecki, G., Sold for $129.99, purchased for $1.00.

*The Golfer and the Millionaire: It's about Having the Drive to Succeed*, by Fisher, Mark, Sold for $94.10, purchased for $0.99.

*Seepage, Drainage and Flow Nets*, by Cedergren, Harry R., Sold for $92.99, purchased for $1.00.

*Jenny and the Jaws of Life*, by Willett, Jincy, Sold for $81.00, purchased for $1.00.

*Wind Energy Comes of Age*, by Gipe, Paul, Sold for $76.00, purchased for $4.00.

*Introduction to Animal Behavior*, by Siiter, Roland J., Sold for $74.99, purchased for $1.99.

*Star Wars Starships of the Galaxy*, by Stephens, Owen K. C., Sold for $67.99, purchased for $1.80.

*Machine Learning*, by Mitchell, Thomas, Sold for $50.99, purchased for $1.00.

*Tamerlane: The Earth Shaker*, by Lamb, Harold, Sold for $50.04, purchased for $1.00.

*Instructor's Manual to Accompany Conceptual Physics, Sixth Edition*, by Hewitt, Paul G., Sold for $50.04, purchased for $1.00.

This is by no means an all inclusive list of my top dollar sellers, I just wanted to demonstrate a cross-section of the odd and unusual so you would see that there is no central theme other than "unusual."

# Where To Sell Your Books

This is the one topic that tends to generate the most controversy among the online bookseller community. There are five dominant marketplaces that list the inventory of over 95% of all books for sale online, Amazon.com, Abebooks.com, Alibris.com, Half.com, and eBay.com.

In the recent past you could choose either Alibris.com or Abebooks.com as your principle marketplace listing service and still have your books sell through Half.com and Amazon.com through bookseller affiliate programs. As a bookseller this was great because you only had to pay a subscription-listing fee to one and still sell through the others. Late last year Amazon.com cancelled their affiliate programs, so now in order to sell books through Amazon.com you must be a subscribed seller. Since I was selling six books through Amazon.com for every book sold elsewhere, signing up to sell through Amazon.com was a no-brainer for me. They are the goliaths of the online marketplaces and a Pro Merchant account for $39.99 per month is a cheap price to have my entire inventory listed on the premier online marketplace. If you are going to pick only one online marketplace to list your book inventory, I strongly encourage you to consider Amazon.com.

Currently I subscribe to use the services of Amazon.com, Alibris.com, and Abebooks.com. The total cost is about $100 per month, but there are advantages and benefits to each.

Rather than focusing on what I do, I would like to describe each of the principal services and let you decide which service or services would best suit your needs.

## Amazon.com

Amazon.com is by far the biggest of the online marketplaces. New subscribers are charged $19.99 a month for the first two months on a trial service and $39.99 for continued service for a Pro Merchant account.

There are some great advantages to selling through Amazon.com; the number of book sales is the dominant one. As I have said before, the majority of my online sales are through Amazon.com.

Amazon.com also has a feedback system where buyers and sellers can rate each other. This can be very helpful to a buyer looking at your listing - if you have a good feedback rating, i.e., if previous buyers have had good things to say about you. This is where adequate and honest listing descriptions can have a very positive effect on your sales.

In addition to your listing description, Amazon.com will charge you 15% of the sale price to cover their cost of processing credit cards and commission on the sale listing, and $1.23 of the shipping and handling fees they charge the buyer.

The fees charged by Amazon.com are transparent to me - and most other online sellers - because they are deducted from payments owed to me before Amazon.com sends funds to my bank, and the payments are direct deposited each two weeks.

There are not many drawbacks to selling through Amazon.com, but data entry and database uploading would be a great inconvenience to me if I were doing these things directly through Amazon.com. This is due in part to the fact that I use a database provided by another marketplace that does not upload listings in the correct format for Amazon.com listing. At the same time, there are thousands of other sellers that use nothing but Amazon.com and they manage.

Another characteristic about Amazon.com that is both an advantage and a disadvantage is navigating through your account. It doesn't seem to matter what I want to see in my account, I always seem to need to enter my password to see anything else. This is a great inconvenience, and at the same time a great assurance of their security.

Another disadvantage to selling through Amazon.com is that you cannot adjust your shipping rates or refuse a sale because a book is too big or too heavy to ship for the reimbursement Amazon.com gives you. As a bookseller, Amazon.com will reimburse you $2.26 for USPS Media Mail orders, $5.05 for USPS Priority Mail® orders, and $7.79 for international orders - period.

In short, the advantages to listing through Amazon.com far outweigh the disadvantages and I highly recommend the Amazon.com marketplace to anyone thinking of getting into the business.

You can read all about becoming an Amazon.com Pro Merchant at:

http://www.amazon.com/exec/obidos/tg/browse/-/1161232/104-1101555-6730319

Just scroll down to where they provide a hyperlink to learn more about the Pro Merchant Services account.

And if this link does not work, just visit Amazon.com, select "Sell Your Stuff," and then the link to reading more about becoming an Amazon.com Pro Merchant.

As a bookseller, one annoyance of Amazon.com is their apparent disregard for booksellers. Every time the United States Postal Service raises the postage rates the independent booksellers on Amazon.com absorb the entire cost. Amazon.com takes forever to adjust the shipping and handling charges paid by buyers and they continue to keep their $1.23, i.e., the increase in postage rates results in losses to the booksellers while the customers get their books shipped at the same cost and Amazon.com gets their same cut.

Fortunately, Amazon holds an annual independent booksellers conference at which all of us independents can voice our discontent with their policy of maintaining a constant shipping charge to the buyers, and keeping the same cut for themselves, while expecting us little guys to absorb the increases in postal rates.

A recent development, or perhaps I should say rumor, is that Amazon will be offering a bookselling program that allows online booksellers to ship their books to Amazon for storage and order fulfillment. At first this might sound great, but you can be sure it is going to cost you. So far, experienced Amazon booksellers have responded with an almost unanimous negative reply. Some of the reasons that booksellers do not like the sound of this include:

1) If a bookseller ships their books to Amazon to be stored in an Amazon warehouse and shipped by Amazon at the time of sale, the bookseller cannot list the book elsewhere and this limits the bookseller's ability to generate revenues through other marketplaces.

2) There almost certainly be additional fees charged by Amazon that are in addition to their current 15% sales commission, and at present, these fees are unknown.

3) The time that Amazon will store the books will almost certainly be limited before the bookseller has to start paying storage fees.

4) The disposition of the books that do not sell is not known, i.e., after some "free" storage period, when Amazon starts tacking on a storage fee, how will the bookseller get his/her inventory back, and who will pay the shipping?

5) When the books are initially sent to Amazon, they will be sent at the bookseller's expense without any reimbursement, and when any given book sells, it appears that only Amazon will getting the shipping costs, i.e., there would not be a shipping reimbursement to the bookseller.

6) Presumably, the bookseller would have to do all the book cleaning and preparation work before shipping the book to Amazon. I don't know about other booksellers, but I do not invest my time in price sticker removal and book cleaning until the book sells; I just don't see much point in putting any time into cleaning them to store on my shelves awaiting a buyer.

7) Booksellers are reluctant to give up the control of their higher priced books to Amazon.

I really do not see this program, currently being tested by a few volunteer Amazon merchants as the "Fulfilled by Amazon" program, gaining much momentum. I do see that it might be attractive to those people that would otherwise consider some sort of consignment arrangement, e.g., college students trying to recover some of their textbook investment, persons with a large personal library that they want to sell, etc.


## Abebooks.com

This is where online bookselling started for me. Abebooks.com is a Canadian company and started out as the greatest rival to Amazon.com.

Among the biggest advantages of Abebooks.com is the software, Homebase, which they will provide free to keep your inventory. The software will fill in most book specific information after you provide an ISBN number with the simple click of the mouse. There are also fields for all other listing information. You do not even need to subscribe to Abebooks.com to get this software, but they have some other advantages that most other online marketplaces do not have.

At Abebooks.com you can adjust your shipping rates within preset limits to charge what you want for shipping domestically and internationally and they charge you a lesser subscription rate and commission that many of the other online marketplaces. The catch is that not as many books will sell through Abebooks.com. Because Abebooks.com allows me to set my own shipping rates, I sell internationally exclusively through them.[11] I have had a few international customers complain about my $14.00 Economy (Surface) Letter Post and/or my $22.00 Priority Mail® rates, but when I explain that it averages out, they understand. Sometimes I will charge $14.00 to send a book that actually only costs $4.50 to send, but other times I will collect $14.00 in shipping and the book will cost me $25.00 to send.

Still, I maintain my Abebooks.com listing subscription and it has been profitable.[12]

You can visit their website and read about listing with them at:

http://abebooks.com/docs/Sell/

They provide direct deposit for your proceeds on a weeky basis.

Through the years I have had very little problem with Abebooks.com, but from my perspective, their devotion to their booksellers and the service they provide has gone downhill. I recently sold a book through Abebooks.com that I had never entered an ISBN number for. Abebooks.com, through their attempt to "help" market books, had matched the title and author to a book that closely resembled mine which had an ISBN number, so they added the ISBN number to my listing. I didn't check all the listing data before shipping the book and ended up having to accept the return, fully reimburse the customer for the purchase and shipping, and pay for return shipping. In all, I was out about $10 because Abebooks.com had altered my listing information and they were unwilling to reimburse me for a mistake they made. This didn't and does not seem right to me, but I have sold many books through Abebooks.com and still maintain my listing subscription with them, just be careful with sales through Abebooks.com and check to see if they have "enhanced" your listing before you process a sale.

If you sell internationally through Abebooks.com, it is a good idea to let your international customers know when their book is shipping and when they might expect to receive it. Australian orders are notorious for arriving at a date well

---

[11] This has changed since my publication in CD-ROM format and I now sell internationally through Amazon as well.

[12] By the time this book goes to print, I will have cancelled my Abebooks marketplace account because the number of sales I get through it no longer justifies spending the money for their marketplace subscription and Amazon has made international bookselling easier.

beyond the quoted delivery times. In fact, last year I had 47 books ship to Australia and only 9 arrived within the quoted delivery times. One was 60 days past due and I refunded the customer only to learn she got the book the next day. It was quite a hassle, but the customer insisted on paying me because I was so friendly and responsive to her inquiries. I ended up having to re-list the book so she could buy it again.

## Alibris.com

Alibris.com is my personal favorite listing service. I have only been listing directly with Alibris.com for about two years, but there is nothing about their service that I do not like. When Amazon.com stopped allowing affiliate listings, Alibris.com made arrangements with Amazon.com to still allow booksellers to update their inventory records on Amazon.com through Alibris.com, and to process their Amazon.com sales through their Alibris.com accounts. They continue to do this at no charge to the bookseller community. [13]

Another great feature of the Alibris.com marketplace is their affiliation with libraries. Alibris.com regularly purchases books from me that they in turn sell to other customers, principally libraries. Books sold and shipped to Alibris.com are shipped postage due using stickers provided by Alibris.com.

One of my favorite features of Alibris.com is their policy of keeping books that customers return because they changed their mind. All of the other marketplaces require the bookseller to issue the customer a full refund for books that are returned for any reason as well as shipping charges. If a customer returns a book to Alibris.com because the customer changed his/her mind, the shipment was a little late; the book wasn't what the customer expected, or any reason other than the book not being in the condition described, Alibris.com will not charge the bookseller. This is a valid policy for all books priced less than $100.

On May 8, 2006, Alibris announced that they have been acquired by Oak Hill Capital Partners and indicated that the acquisition should bode well for their plans of expansion, including their international presence. They also stated that, "Our partnership with Oak Hill will help us fulfill our commitment to making Alibris sellers the most successful in the online world." I guess only time will tell, but in my own humble opinion, the potential cash infusion can't hurt.

---

[13] This is no longer true. After Amazon ended their affiliate programs, Alibris offered to maintain their inventory uploads and the processing of Amazon orders through their Alibris accounts. This turned out to be a temporary practice only, Alibris now charges booksellers $0.25 for every Amazon order processed through their Alibris account. A quarter doesn't sound like much, but if you sell 400 books a month through Amazon and process the orders through Alibris, they will deduct $100 a month from your account for doing something that it fully automated. I have opted to maintain my Alibris account and I process my Amazon orders through them because I cancelled my Abebooks account. Letting Alibris handle the processing of my Amazon sales assures me that I will not be selling a book on two marketplaces and having to cancel one order, thus taking a fulfillment ration hit.

Hands down, Alibris.com is my personal favorite bookselling marketplace.[14] If they generated the sales volumes that I get through Amazon.com, I would list through them exclusively.

You can read all about becoming a seller through Alibris.com at:

http://sellers.alibris.com/

And selecting the "Learn More!" option.

I am just beginning to get into selling things other than books, like books on tape, CD's, DVD's and records, all of which can be marketed and sold through Alibris.com, as well as e-books.

## The Other Online Marketplaces

There are a number of other online marketplaces that you can list and sell books through, and before you pick one for yourself, I suggest that you look them over too. They include:

BarnesadNoble.com
Half.com
eBay.com

The first two of which you can subscribe to as an affiliate through Abebooks.com and/or Alibris.com. eBay.com is a different story altogether.

## eBay.com

EBay.com is quickly becoming a formidable venue for selling books (and all kinds of other things), in fact, for many things eBay.com is leading the marketplace. Many booksellers that deal in collectibles and/or collections by series or authors, find eBay.com the best place to market their books, but for me it is an awkward and inefficient way to sell my books because each and every book requires that I set up a separate auction and the task of setting up the auction is just too time consuming.

Another reason I have avoided eBay.com is the inconvenience of taking and uploading images of every book I list. Amazon.com and Alibris.com, both provide cover images for most of the books I list that are linked to their respective ISBNs.

I do not want to put eBay.com down because I buy and sell other things through their auction marketplace and I know many other booksellers are devoted to eBay.com marketing. Perhaps your investigation will lead you to a different conclusion for your online bookselling than I have experienced.

---

[14] With their institution of the $0.25 charge for all Amazon orders processed through Alibris, some of what was appealing about the Alibris marketplace to me has been tarnished. I have opted to keep my Alibris account and they are still my favorite marketplace owing to their library purchase program and the thorough bookseller transaction records provided by them.

EBay.com can also be very useful for clearing out your firewood. You can group lots of firewood by theme and sell these lots in separate auctions, quite often recovering much of your firewood investment. If you decide to do this, don't hype your auction with dishonest descriptions. It is not necessary to claim that the books are the firewood you split out of your inventory, but don't claim they are unsorted lots either. Just tell people what the books are, their condition, and what the shipping costs will be. Let the buyers determine the value of the books in the auction through their bidding. If they don't sell honestly in an auction, you can still write-off the cost of the auction and donate the books to a library for another write-off.

Since the CD-ROM first edition release of this book, eBay has launched a new program for "busy shoppers," eBay Express. To become an eBay Express merchant, you must satisfy the following requirements:

1) You must be an experienced eBay seller and:

    a. Have an eBay public profile that shows a minimum of 100 feedback comments from buyers, 98% of which must be positive.

    b. List your items for sale in a Fixed Price or Store inventory format.

    c. When you list your item for sale you must make sure you include a photograph, the condition of the item via "Item Specifics," and provide the customer shipping costs in the shipping fields.

2) You must become a PayPal Premier or PayPal Business merchant.

I do see some advantages to this new selling venue on eBay, but with respect to used bookselling, it offers nothing new, in fact, eBay Express is not for used items, it is only for new items.

If you want to know more about this eBay program, you can visit:

http://pages.ebay.com/express/service/about/seller-questions.html

# Establishing An Inventory Process And Management System

There are few things you can do before getting started that will aid your success more that organizing your thoughts, goals, and INVENTORY.

There are probably just about as many different ways to organize an inventory, as there are booksellers. I will tell you about a couple, as well as the one I use, but you will need to sit down and think about what you want to do before you get started.

Inventory management is another can of worms that needs to be given some thought before you start spending time entering a bunch of book data and learning that it all needs to be re-entered because your entry method is incompatible with what the marketplaces can accept in an upload.

## Inventory Management

I started with the Homebase database and inventory software provided by Abebooks.com, and this is what I still use today. It is very user friendly and straightforward to use. In most cases the only book information I have to enter is the ISBN number, then I click on ISBN lookup and the database goes out on the Internet and retrieves most of the other relevant book information. Using the provided drop-down menus in the software enters all other information, like the book condition, type, and binding. After I have entered all the books I am managing (initial entry as well as sold books) I simply use the export function to export the updates to a file on my computer. I name the file according to the day of the month, and then I upload this file to my respective marketplaces.

There are booksellers that use elaborate Stock Keeping Unit, SKU, systems, but I have not found this necessary. The Homebase software saves my entries in a numerical SKU order so that I do not have duplicate inventory numbers, and I put a Post-It note on the book with the same number. I then store my inventory in numerical order so that the Post-It is sticking out to be easily read. You could also choose to print no-residue labels in a laser or ink jet printer and stick them on the spines of the books, but Post-Its® are very cheap and stick out like tabs, they leave no residue, and they are very easy to remove.

If you do not want to use the Homebase software I have described, you can enter and store the information in an Excel spreadsheet, just be sure to organize the spreadsheet so that the information can be exported and uploaded to your marketplace of choice. You can get the file requirements from the website of the marketplace you choose to use.

To access Abebooks.com and download their free Homebase software, go to:

http://dogbert.abebooks.com/docs/homebase/main.shtml

## Inventory Process

There are a number of ways you can organize your inventory. My son keeps his inventory in alphabetical order by author. There are some that keep their inventories in alphabetical order by title, and there are others that keep their inventory in boxed lots according to when they were entered for sale. The problems I see with these methods is in shelving and a need to make room for a new book necessitating moving perhaps dozens of other books already on the shelf.

Personally, all of these methods sound time consuming to me and they require too much handling and sorting. As I enter my books in my database, they are assigned a numerical inventory number by the database. I write this number on a Post-It note and stick it on the book so that the Post-It is readable when I put the book on the shelf. Then when I have a stack of books ready to be shelved I put them at the end of my inventory and do not have to do any further sorting. Since all of my books are numerically shelved it is very easy to find one when it sells and I only need to take a list of sold book inventory numbers to the shelves to find the books I have sold and do not need to write down titles, authors, or box numbers to take with me to the shelves. The only drawback that I see to my system is that after I have listed 999,999 books I will need to start the numbering over or contact Abebooks.com about adding a digit to my software because the software only allows for up to 999,999 books to be entered. I am not too concerned about reaching this limit any time soon. Of course, as I sell books, there are holes left on the shelves that require me to go through my shelves each couple months and move the books to fill the gaps. When I do this, it only amounts to sliding the books over and moving books up from the next shelf. I still maintain the same numerical order, but now rather than gaps in the shelves, there are only gaps in the numbers.

When you are mapping out an inventory process, don't forget that basements sometimes flood with a few inches of water and every book that is on the floor is going to be destroyed and a lot heavier to haul out of your basement to the trash.

I also want to emphasize once again the danger of a bookshelf full of books falling on a child, if children are going to be around your inventory, make sure the shelves will not tip over on a child climbing them – or better yet, don't even keep your books where children can even contemplate climbing them.

# Storing Your Inventory

Unless you really trust your pets, keep your inventory and them separated. Used books have all kinds of intriguing odors for the furry members of your family, and some of these smells just might excite them enough that they keep the lower shelves well watered. We have cats in our house and every time I bring a new load of books home, the cats check them out thoroughly. I have even seen my cats get into a bag of books and roll around. Since they are female cats, they do not mark the new books as belonging to them, but to get to the books to smell them I have seen them tear into a bag, so I do not let them around my books because I do not want a $100 book to be clawed and destroyed. Having previously been a servant to a dog, I suspect they could do a lot more damage very quickly.

As I discussed earlier, you should also layout your inventory in a manner that makes finding and accessing your books easy. You do not want to be in a position of constantly moving your inventory around and you certainly won't want to spend a half hour finding each book you sell.

There are potential tax deduction implications as well. If you intend to take a deduction for the business use of your home, you must dedicate an area of your house to your online bookselling business and use that area exclusively for that business.

I believe we have covered most other items of interest regarding the storing of your inventory in other parts of this book, and I so not want to be redundant.

# Attention To Detail And Customer Satisfaction

Online bookselling has many rules imposed by the various marketplaces, and one of the common rules to almost all of them is that a customer can return a book he or she is not happy with and the bookseller must refund the entire purchase price, the shipping fee, and in some cases the return-shipping fee.

Booksellers are also responsible for refunding book purchases and shipping fees for any books that never make it to the buyer.

Thus, there should be motivation to deliver a book that the customer will be happy getting. To do this consistently requires that you:

1) Always grade your books accurately.

2) Note book defects and/or blemishes that might be viewed by a customer as making it worth less.

3) Keep on top of your inventory and make sure you do not sell a book that has already been sold.

4) Process all of your orders in a timely manner.

5) Ship books within 48 hours of receiving an order (preferably within one business day).

6) Pack the books so they do not get damaged or lost in the mail.

7) Cover yourself by adding delivery confirmation and/or insurance to more valuable shipments.

8) If the marketplace through which a book is ordered has a feedback system be sure to leave prompt and positive feedback for your buyers.

9) Approximately two weeks after a book is shipped, if the buyer has not left feedback for you, you can send them a friendly email and ask that they leave appropriate feedback, or include a letter like the following with your shipment:

Dear [Marketplace Name] Book Buyer,

[Your bookstore name] would like to thank you for your recent purchase and let you know that we have submitted positive buyer feedback for you on [Marketplace Name].

Since the on-line book selling business is so competitive and we are new to direct sales through [Marketplace Name], we would appreciate your feedback regarding your purchase from [Your bookstore name]. We know the choice of purchasing from us may have been influenced to some extent on our [Marketplace Name] feedback rating and/or your belief that if we are new, we must be trying to provide quality books at reasonable prices, but the truth is that many buyers do not even consider purchasing from [Marketplace Name] dealers unless the seller has a positive feedback history. This combined with the fact that we are new sellers on [Marketplace Name] makes it even more important to us that you provide us with your feedback.

If for any reason you are dissatisfied with your purchase or our service, we would like the opportunity to resolve the issue before you post neutral or negative feedback. At [Your bookstore name] we work hard to comply with the [Marketplace Name] return policies and make every effort to surpass them with our customers. So, if you have a reason that you feel justifies a neutral or negative feedback about us, please contact us and give us the opportunity to make you a satisfied customer.

We hope you are happy with your purchase and that you will remember us when you make any future on-line purchases through [Marketplace Name], and we want to thank you in advance for taking the time to post your [Marketplace Name] feedback.

Best Regards,

[Your Bookstore Name]

If you do decide to solicit feedback by emailing your customers, use caution and:

1) Do not solicit feedback more than one time. If the customer still doesn't provide you with feedback they probably aren't going to and may get annoyed if you keep asking them for it. Multiple email solicitations for feedback may result in negative feedback.

2) If you solicit feedback too soon, i.e., before the customer even gets their book, you run the risk of being graded for the performance of the post office. Despite the customer choosing standard delivery, i.e., Media Mail®, when they placed their order, they are likely to leave feedback to the effect that delivery was too slow when the book arrives after 10 days even though Media Mail® guarantees only 4 - 14 business days. Don't run the risk of encouraging such feedback by reminding your customers their book has not arrived yet by sending them a premature solicitation for feedback.

I don't think many customers give much thought to giving feedback or what it means to you as a bookseller, but they are very judgmental when they read what others have to say about you. Don't give them reason to judge you based on the performance of the post office, but do include something with your book shipment to them that reminds them to leave you feedback. Tactfully done, this can result in a lot of positive feedback.

Customer inquiries and questions are another subject that warrants attention. Be prompt, courteous, professional, and consistent. I do not think that any of these tips is more valuable than being prompt, particularly if a customer is asking where their shipment is or why it isn't in the condition they expected. From the customer's perspective, their question is a crisis and they expect you to get back to them quickly, if you don't, they get even more anxious and believe you are trying to pull one over their head. Many customers already believe you are part of a scam or they are at least skeptical of the entire online business community.

If I get an email from a customer and I am away from home and unable to get their answer immediately, I will still send them an immediate response to let them know that I will get back to them with an answer as soon as I can. This relieves their anxiety and lets them know I care about giving them an answer.

Develop your own policies and stick to them consistently. The online marketplaces will minimally mandate most policies, but those within your control should be developed and adhered to with consistency.

If a customer does leave you negative feedback on Amazon.com, it is usually worth the effort to ask them to remove it. Most negative feedback is left for deliveries that take longer than the customer expected owing to delays by the post office, but some arrive within the quoted delivery times and the customer didn't realize that 4 – 14 days for standard delivery could take two weeks – go figure.

If you do get negative feedback for delayed deliveries, you might try emailing a letter like the following to the customer to see if they will remove the negative feedback. I know it is tempting to tell them they are an idiot for choosing a standard delivery when they needed the book for a class in three days, but you probably won't get much cooperation from them if you tell them they are an idiot. Try something a little more diplomatic like the following.

Dear [Buyer's Name],

In reviewing my bookseller feedback I saw that you left negative feedback for me owing to the time your book took to arrive. I apologize for the delay in your book delivery, but I can assure you it was shipped within 24 hours of you placing the order via standard shipping as you specified.

I would be grateful if you would reconsider and remove the negative feedback that is more a grading of the United States Postal Service than the service we provided, i.e., I feel that your negative feedback is more reflective of the post office than me as a bookseller. I am also concerned that other online buyers will see your negative feedback and choose to buy from another bookseller and we will be unjustly punished for the performance of the post office.

If you are willing to remove your feedback, you can easily do so by clicking on the "Your Account" at the Amazon.com home page. Then click on the "View Order" button next to the transaction in which you purchased from us. Then choose the second box down that is labeled "Your Feedback for [our bookstore]." Then you can select the "Remove Feedback" box.

If in the future you need a book quickly, you can choose the expedited delivery option, which will assure you of a Priority Mail® or Air Mail delivery, this option is an extra $2.00.

We appreciate your business and thank you in advance for your consideration of negative feedback removal.


Best Regards,


[Your Name]
[Your BookStore Name]

# Packaging And Shipping

One of the things I learned the hard way was how to overcome the seemingly destructive intent of the US Postal Service. I printed easy to read labels so the US Postal Service would not have any difficulty understanding where I wanted my packages to go. I put all of my books in self-sealing mailers so they would not be accidentally opened, and in general did everything I could to ship every book securely. I even added extra tape to their flat rate Priority Mail envelopes so the seams would not split open, but I still had to refund about 3% of my orders because books never arrived or the envelope arrived without the book I put in it. In the grand scheme of things, the post office does a fantastic job, but all it takes is for them to lose a $100 book and you will become an instant cynic of the postal system.

Three percent of books lost does not sound like much, but it adds up and the more troublesome part is the time it takes to rectify and process these refunds. If you are already an online bookseller, you probably know exactly what I am talking about and it is quite likely that you are experiencing the same frustrations.

My first step in rectifying the problem was to make the US Postal Service pay for their mistakes by taking out insurance on the more valuable books, those in the $15+ range. The logic was that if they lost a book I had insured, they would pay for it. Seems like a reasonable assumption doesn't it? Well, collecting on insurance from the US Postal Service is a real test in patience.

First you have to show that what they lost was worth what you are claiming. This did not seem to me like it would be a difficult thing to do; after all, I had an invoice copy, which showed exactly what I had been paid for the book. Guess what, they don't care how much you sold the book for, they only care how much you paid for it, i.e., what was your financial loss. So much for my assumed rational logic. The real kicker is that it can take anywhere from six months to a year to actually get paid by the US Postal Service on the insurance claim.

All this solution concept seemed to do was add frustration, cost, and stress to me. There had to be a better way, and believe it or not, a postal carrier gave me a few tips about how I could minimize the probability of "occurrences."

I have been practicing these tips for the past three years with unbelievable success. I have had only ONE book get lost for every 3,350 shipped through the US Postal Service. That is a loss rate of just under 0.03%. These simple tips have reduced my "Postal" losses by two orders of magnitude to almost nothing.

If you are an online bookseller and you bought this book looking for a few tips to improve your bottom line, following these simple tips could pay for this book very quickly.

I don't want to confuse things by listing these tips here, I want to include them in my step-by-step packing instructions, but I will emphasize them in the instructions to make them clear.

## Media Mail® Packing

About 85% of all the books I ship are sent by US Postal Service Media Mail®. It is a reduced shipping rate intended to condone the sharing of information and the US Postal Service states the following restrictions on their website:

> "Used for books, film, manuscripts, printed music, printed test materials, sound recordings, play scripts, printed educational charts, loose-leaf pages and binders consisting of medical information, videotapes, and computer-recorded media such as CD-ROMs and diskettes. Media Mail cannot contain advertising."

The down side to shipping by US Postal Service Media Mail® is the delivery time, 4 - 14 days, but it is apparent that shipping books does qualify.

Like most other online booksellers, I opted to purchase self-sealing bubble pack envelopes to ship my books because they were relatively inexpensive, they provided protection for the books, and I could get them in different sizes to accommodate different sized books. Since none of the online marketplaces pay booksellers enough in shipping reimbursements to buy boxes or to ship in post office priority boxes, self-sealing bubble pack envelopes seemed to be the only viable option. I still use them today, and I pack all of my Media Mail® shipments according to the following step-by-step instructions and accompanying photographs.

1)  Remove all price stickers and markings from the book.

   a. There are few exceptions to the sticker removal that I allow. If I am selling an ex-library book, my listing will state that it is an ex-library book and in many cases I will leave the library-cataloguing sticker on the book because any attempt to remove it will generally result in some substantial damage to the book.

   b. There are not many things you can do to annoy a customer more than leaving a price sticker on a book that shows them you paid a dollar for a book that you are selling them for $100. The customer does not need to know what you paid for the book and you are better off removing all evidence of the price you paid.

   c. When removing price stickers from books, take care to avoid damaging the surface of the book. I use a small hard plastic scraper to scrape them off, but even this can damage a book's cover if you get carried away.

   d. Use a cleaner that will not remove the finish from the book. One that I have found to be quite good at removing the sticker residue and for generally cleaning book covers and dust jackets is Goo Gone®. Be careful not to get it on the pages of the book as it will soak into unfinished paper, but it is excellent for the covers of most books including glossy finished covers on paperbacks. It also leaves a scent of orange. You might also try rubbing alcohol.

e.  To remove stubborn stickers, put a few drops of Goo Gone® or rubbing alcohol on the sticker and allow it to soak for a few minutes before trying to remove the sticker. This will partially dissolve the sticker adhesive and make removal easier.

f.  Don't just remove stickers and price markings clean the entire cover of the book. Use a paper towel with Goo Gone® or rubbing alcohol and wipe off the entire cover. If you send a customer a dirty and/or grimy book they ARE going to notice.

Part of cleaning up books for shipment should include leafing through it and removing papers, notes, receipts, and money. As strange as it may sound, people do leave money in books they donate. I have found several books with dollar bills in them and once found one with a $20 bill in it. I understood the book with the $20 bill in it because it also had a gift inscription written on the first blank wishing a grandchild a happy birthday and the $20 must have been an additional part of the intended gift, but the only reason I can attribute to the one dollar bills I have found is people using dollar bills as bookmarks.

In any case, it is nice to find a dollar inside a book you only paid a quarter for, and it is really nice to find a $20 bill in a book you paid $0.49 for.

Incidentally, I did try to recall where I bought the book with the $20 in it, but I had this book in my inventory long enough that I could not trace it back to the store or book sale I bought it at. In the past two years I have been making a point of tracking purchase lots to zero in on which sources are the most profitable, how long it takes me to recover my investment from any given lot purchased, and which sources tend to yield the highest value per book.

2)  Cut out the shipping information and tape it to the shipping envelope. Don't be cheap tape it well.

a.  Using address labels will result in lost books because the labels will get peeled off the envelopes by the postal machines or if you use an ink jet printer and the label gets wet, the ink will run and the label cannot be read. Tip: if you use adhesive labels, tape over them so they do not get peeled off the envelope.

b.  Tip: run the tape down well. I use a Bondo® blade to make sure the tape gets stuck down to the envelope well. It only takes one swipe of the Bondo® blade to run the tape down well and remove almost all of the trapped air bubbles. You can buy a Bondo® blade for about a buck at most automotive supply stores.

Position address label (standard envelope shown, but method is same for self-sealing bubble pack envelopes)

Tape the label down well using 2" clear packing tape (black duct tape used in photo so it would be visible) and stamp Media Mail®.

I had a Media Mail® stamp made for my convenience and to speed things up at the post office.

"Media Mail"® stamped on clean newsprint paper.

I also had an "Economy (Surface) Letter Post" stamp made for international book shipments.

"Economy (Surface) Letter Post" stamped on clean newsprint.

3) Wrap the book in clean newsprint and put the book in the envelope and seal it. If the book is a new or valuable book, wrap it in 2" shrink-wrap before wrapping it in clean newsprint and putting it in the envelope with the customer's packing invoice copy folded to show on the cover of the book. This will look more professional to the customer when they open the envelope and will offer additional moisture protection for the book.

A book shown wrapped in clean newsprint.

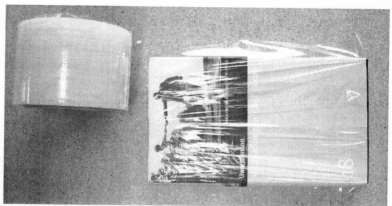

Shrink wrapping a book for shipment.

a.   Do not try to stuff the book in the envelope.  Self-sealing bubble pack
     envelopes are not Kevlar®, they will split at the seams if the book fits
     too tightly.  Choose an envelope size that does not test the limits of the
     envelope.

b.   Tip: do not trust the self-sealing adhesive, put a strip of 2" cellophane
     tape across the flap too, and run it down with your Bondo® blade.

9 3

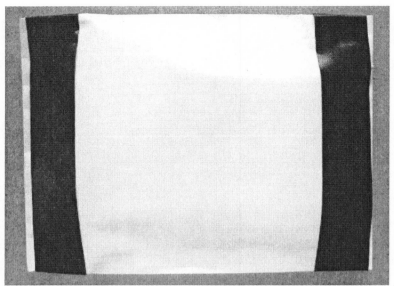

Taped end flaps as seen from back of envelope.

Taped flaps as seen from front view.

c.  Tip: if the book is a large or heavy hardcover with sharp corners on the cover, wrap the entire envelope with strips of 2" cellophane packing tape to reinforce the envelope, this will help to keep the book from escaping before it gets to its destination.

Cross-taping as seen from back of envelope.

Cross-taping "Ready To Go" envelope as viewed from front of envelope. Again, black tape used for visibility in photo only.

4) Stamp the envelope "Media Mail"® or write this on the envelope in 1" letters. I showed this in the first step, but you want to check that it has been stamped.

Look over the captioned photographs of the Media Mail® packing that I have included. I intentionally used a black 2" tape to show where I use 2" cellophane tape so that it would show up in the photograph.

Do not risk putting books in 10" x 13" standard envelopes unless they are thin and lightweight. Even though many books will fit in these envelopes, they are likely to get damaged and/or tear through the envelope if they are too big or too heavy. The post office does not handle mail very carefully and many times packages are tossed into sorting bins with other heavier things thrown in on top. Use a self-sealing bubble envelope if you are in doubt, or purchase book mailing corrugated book folds.

---

### Personal Experience

Before I started my online bookselling business I imported ceramic figures and pottery from the Czech Republic.

All of my purchased products were double boxed and strapped down to pallets before being sent to me by airfreight. We would check our inventory in and sort it by product before marketing it.

Out of 750 boxes shipped to us, we had three pieces get broken.

When a customer would buy a figure from us we would wrap it in a three inch cushion of bubble wrap inside a very heavy double-wall cardboard box filled with shredded paper; and only put one item in each box.

The post office consistently broke 65% of everything we shipped. The *boxes* were not appreciably damaged on inspection, but the post office still managed to break the majority of what we shipped.

All I have been able to determine is that they must drop every box from a ten story building so that it lands flat on one side to minimize evidence of external box damage. By doing this, everything inside the box is subjected to hundreds of g's on impact and is broken by its own mass. That way the post office can deliver a box with minimal evidence of external handling abuse and still manage to break almost everything inside.

By marking the box **"FRAGILE"** you could be assured of a twenty-story drop test.

---

## Priority Mail® Packing

There are two methods of US Postal Service Priority Mail® that I use, Priority Mail Flat-Rate Envelopes and Priority Mail Flat-Rate Boxes.

I use the US Postal Service Priority Mail Flat-Rate Envelopes for books that fit comfortably in the envelope and the Priority Mail Flat-Rate Boxes for those books that simply will not fit in the Priority Mail Flat-Rate Envelopes. I have described the packing method that I use for each separately.

A US Postal Service Priority Mail Flat-Rate Envelope.

All of the supplies for using this service are available free at your US Post Office, but the free supplies have consequences. The envelopes are not very durable and tend to come apart at the seams when postal carriers handle them roughly and they are experts at rough handling.

The trick to keeping your books from escaping from these envelopes is to attach the envelope to the book and this is one of the greatest tips I got from a postal carrier.

1)  Put your book and the customer's invoice copy in a US Postal Service Priority Mail® or Express Mail® envelope. These envelopes are available free and have a reinforcement fiber woven into the paper. This reinforced envelope is shown later with the book inside it, and I will note it for you then.

A reinforced "Express Mail"® envelope. This type of envelope is also available in "Global Priority" and "Priority," and it doesn't matter which you use because it is only to secure your book inside the mailing envelope.

2)  Weigh the book in the protective envelope with the US Postal Service Priority Mail Flat-Rate Envelope.

3)  Log into your USPS.com account and enter your customer's address, the package weight, and the other requested information. If you do not have an account, you can sign up for a Click N Ship® account at the Click N Ship® URL provided in Appendix A.

4)  Print out your Click N Ship® label information.

5)  Cut out the Click N Ship® label information along with the printed Delivery Confirmation. Retain the lower half for your records.

6)  Using a glue stick, glue the label and Delivery Confirmation to the US Postal Service Priority Mail Flat-Rate Envelope.

Position and glue the Click N Ship® label and the Delivery Confirmation Label. Shown here positioned and glued only.

7)  Cover the glued on label and Delivery Confirmation with 2" clear cellophane packing tape and run the tape down good. Be careful not to tape the seams of the envelope because the post office gets bent out of shape if they think your tape is reinforcing the seams of their envelopes.

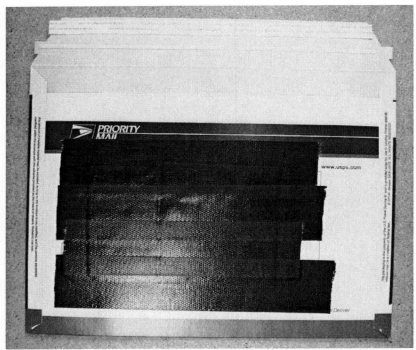

Tape and run down the labels using 2" clear cellophane packing tape. Do not tape the edges of the US Postal Service Priority Mail Flat-Rate Envelope; they do not want you to reinforce their envelopes. In fact, the post office would prefer that you use a Priority Mail Flat-Rate Box if their Priority Mail Flat-Rate Envelope is not sufficiently strong for your books, but this is expensive.

8)   Slip the book with protective envelope into the US Postal Service Priority Mail Flat-Rate Envelope.

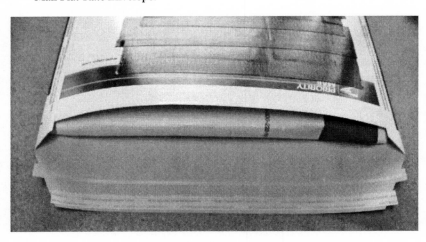

Slip the book (inside a reinforced envelope) into the Priority Mail Flat-Rate Envelope.

9)   Tip: Tape the book inside the protective envelope to the inside of the US Postal Service Priority Mail Flat-Rate Envelope.   I have included photographs of this where I have purposely split the mailing envelope along the seams to show how the book and protective envelope are taped inside the mailing envelope.   I also used a black tape that will show up in the photograph instead of clear cellophane tape.

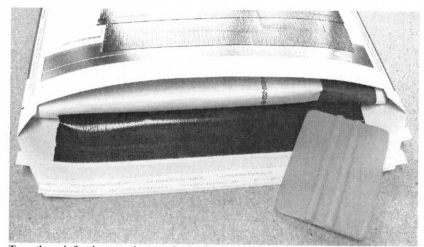

Tape the reinforcing envelope to the back of the Priority Mail Flat-Rate Envelope and make sure it is run down with a Bondo® blade so it sticks well.

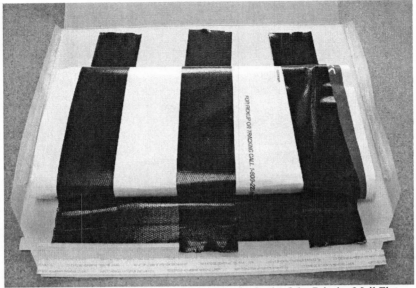

Cut lengths of tape and tape across the book to the back of the Priority Mail Flat-Rate Envelope. I split the Priority Mail Flat-Rate Envelope here so you could see how I tape the book (which is secure inside a reinforced envelope) to the Priority Mail Flat-Rate Envelope. If you first attach the tape to the flap, you can hold the Priority Mail Flat-Rate Envelope open and tape across the book to the bottom of the envelope.

10) Tip: Before closing the US Postal Service Priority Mail Flat-Rate Envelope, tape the upper lip to the lower lip (the lower lip I am referring to is the one with the flap that seals the envelope) and to the book. I have also included a photograph of this step.

Now tape the front flap of the Priority Mail Flat-Rate Envelope to both the book and the other tape, thus securing the front and back to the book.

11) Close and seal the US Postal Service Priority Mail Flat-Rate Envelope using the self-adhesive on the closure flap.

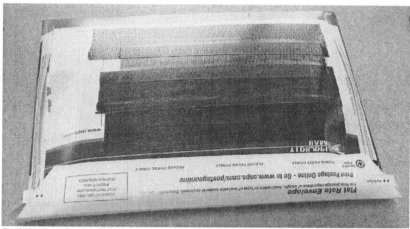

Seal the envelope using the integral self-sealing flap.

12) Tip: Run a single strip of 2" clear cellophane tape across the flap and the easy open strip of the US Postal Service Priority Mail Flat-Rate Envelope.

Tape across the self-sealing flap. Note: I have found some post office branches that will not allow this strip of tape. I guess they are once again promoting the use of Priority Mail Flat-Rate Boxes. Check with the post office you will be using to see if they will allow this strip of tape.

If you will follow these steps when preparing books for shipment via Priority Mail Flat-Rate Envelope, you will greatly reduce the number of books that the post office loses owing to splitting of the Priority Mail Flat-Rate Envelopes and escaping books. Even if the seams split, your book will be protected and the address will be attached to the book and the protective envelope.

I have had several customers comment about how difficult it can be to get their book out of a Priority Mail Flat-Rate Envelope that I have packed, but they thanked me for taking the time to make sure their book was well packed and not lost.

## Additional Cost Saving Packaging Options

For those paperbacks that will fit very comfortably in a plain old manila envelope, you can pack and ship them like this via Media Mail® if you take a few precautions.

1) You should wrap them well in a clean news print paper or bubble wrap to help protect them. I would not suggest newspaper because it can transfer ink to the covers of the book you are shipping and upset your customer. You can buy unprinted newsprint paper at most industrial office supply stores, or you can get butcher paper by the roll at most consumer discount warehouses, e.g., Costco®, or Sam's Club®. Shipping books this way really cuts down on the cost per book for shipping materials.

2) After the envelope is addressed and the book is inside, reinforce the envelope with 2" cellophane packing tape (see earlier photo). Even a relatively lightweight book is capable of escaping from an ordinary envelope if minimal precautions are not taken.

This method of packing your lightweight books can have a profound impact on your bottom line. From my own experience I have found self-sealing bubble pack envelopes to cost around $0.42 on average (based on my usage of #0, #1, #2, #3, #4, #5, & #6 sizes and the quantities of each I use) at an office supply store, and that is about twice what you will pay if you buy cases of 100 like I do from an industrial supply wholesaler. The average cost of 10" x 13" quality-mailing envelopes is much less, about $0.15 per envelope at Costco®, and there are even lower quality envelopes that you can buy in the $0.10 per envelope range. The cost difference does not sound like all that much, but if you are selling 500 books per month and saving $0.33 per book on shipping supplies, it adds up to $1,980 a year!

Shipping books like this will not work for all the books you sell, but of the books I sell, approximately 45% of them can be safely and securely shipped in a regular envelope with clean newsprint paper wrapping.

## Priority Mail Flat-Rate Boxes and Global Priority Envelope Shipping

Packing for both of these shipping methods is very similar. In the case of the Priority Mail Flat-Rate Box, just make sure the book is secured inside the box with tape and that the empty space is filled with crushed clean newsprint or bubble wrap so that the book is not free to slide around inside the box.

Global Priority mailing envelopes are the same size and quality as Priority Mail Flat-Rate Envelopes. The packing is identical except for the addressing of the envelope. Write all of the address information on a Global Priority Mail envelope with a black Sharpie® and then tape over the writing with clear 2" cellophane tape to avoid the ink getting smudged. You will also need to complete a Customs Declaration form and affix it with the self-sticking adhesive to the Global Priority envelope.

## Establish A Packing Process

In preparing your books for shipment it is important that you establish a process (or routine if you prefer) and stick to it.

Pulling your sold books from your inventory and packing them for shipment is not rocket science, in fact it gets boring and for this reason alone it is important to have a routine. If you start doing the steps in different order every day, you will probably mix up shipments before long and this will lead to:

1) Additional shipping costs coming out of your pocket.

2) Dissatisfied customers and possibly negative feedback resulting in fewer sales.

2) Books that should have been sold getting returned to your unsold inventory at your expense (you pay for the return postage for customer returns).

4) Frustration and stress

I have chosen the following process and it has worked very well for me. You may choose to alter the steps to suit yourself, but I strongly encourage you to establish an order and stick to it.

1) Print sales invoices

2) Pull books from inventory

3) Remove pricing information, stickers, and thoroughly clean book covers and dust jacket

4) Insert sales invoices (2) inside front cover of each matching book.

5) Then on a book by book basis:

   a. Remove both sales invoices and check that they are the same and match the book they are in

   b. Cut out address information from one invoice and attach to packing envelope.

c.   Check the second copy once again, fold it, and put it inside front cover of book for the customer.

d.   Put the book inside the addressed shipping envelope.

e.   Return to step 5A for next book.

I know it may sound silly, but when you have 35 books all over your packing table, if you don't have a system that works for you, you will inevitably mix up a few books and their correspondingly addressed envelopes, and it will cost you. The mundane tasks of the business warrant attention to the details or they will be a source of lost profits.

# Shipping Methods, Options, And Reimbursements

## Shipping Methods

There is no steadfast rule that dictates the means of shipping to use, but I have not found any means more economical than the US Postal Service.

The majority of my sales are shipped via US Postal Service Media Mail®, Priority Mail®, First Class Mail®, Global Priority Mail, Surface (Economy) Letter Post (international delivery), or Airmail Letter Post (international delivery), but there is the rare customer that requests a Expedited Mail delivery or United Parcel Services® delivery.

When you start researching the online bookselling business you will probably find there are a number of online booksellers that state they ship all orders Priority Mail®. While this sounds great to the customers, it is an unnecessary offering that will cost you. Unless you are specializing in selling books that will command prices high enough to justify doing it, and you are willing to sacrifice some of your profits just to offer Priority Mail service, there is really no reason for sacrificing a big part of your profits just to send your books quicker. Besides, your customers have the option of picking and paying for expedited mail service at the time they place their orders.

In the spreadsheet table below I have demonstrated the differences in the cost of Priority Mail® versus Media Mail® so that you can see that it is possible to lose money in your business by blindly assuming the role of shipping everything via Priority Mail®.

**The assumptions in the table are:**

1) **100 books sold**
2) **7 will qualify for First Class Mail® (5.1 to 6.0 oz.)**
3) **53 will weigh between 6 oz and 16 oz.**
4) **27 will be between 16 oz and 32 oz. (1-2 pounds)**
5) **7 will weigh between 32 oz and 48 oz (2-3 pounds)**
6) **4 will weigh between 48 oz and 64 oz (3-4 pounds)**
7) **2 will weigh between 64 and 80 oz (4-5 pounds)**
8) **Books under a pound can be packed in clean newsprint paper and standard 10" x 13" envelopes, all others could be shipped in self-sealing bubble pack envelopes for an average cost of $0.42 each.**
9) **Books between one pound and 5 pounds can be packed in bubble envelopes, but books in excess of three pounds must be put in Priority Mail Flat-Rate Boxes if you opt to give free upgrades to Priority Mail® services.**
10) **Because this table is intended to show the added cost of using Priority Mail® as a customer incentive, assume that all of these 100 book sales were to be shipped Media Mail® per the customer's choice.**
11) **Assume that all 100 orders are for domestic shipments.**
12) **Assume that all sales were made through Amazon.com where you are given a shipping credit of $2.26 for Media Mail® orders.**

| | Quantity In Each Weight Range | Standard Shipping | Priority Mail® Shipping |
|---|---|---|---|
| First Class | 7 | $11.83 | $28.35 |
| Media Mail® 6.0 oz up to 1.0 pound | 53 | $89.57 | $214.65 |
| Media Mail® 1.0 pound up to 2.0 pounds | 27 | $66.69 | $109.35 |
| Media Mail® 2.0 pound up to 3.0 pounds | 7 | $20.65 | $28.35 |
| Media Mail® 3.0 pound up to 4.0 pounds | 4 | $13.72 | $32.40 |
| Media Mail® 4.0 pound up to 5.0 pounds | 2 | $7.82 | $16.20 |
| | | | |
| Total Shipping | | $210.28 | $429.30 |
| | | | |
| Shipping Reimbursements Received | | $226.00 | |
| | | | |
| Profit Or Loss From Shipping | | $15.72 | -$203.30 |

If you extrapolate this for 350 books per month, you can see just how much shipping costs can add up and how much profit the choice to ship all books via Priority Mail® can cost you over a year.

| | Standard Shipping | Priority Mail® Shipping |
|---|---|---|
| | | |
| Shipping Profit/Loss Per Month | $55.02 | ($711.55) |
| Shipping Profit/Loss Per Year | $660.24 | ($8,538.60) |
| | | |

The difference between choosing to ship via Priority Mail® and shipping by standard mail is $9,198.84, per year, i.e., you can make $660.24 per year using standard shipping methods,

Media Mail®, or it can cost you $8,538.00 to offer the Priority Mail® incentive to your customers.

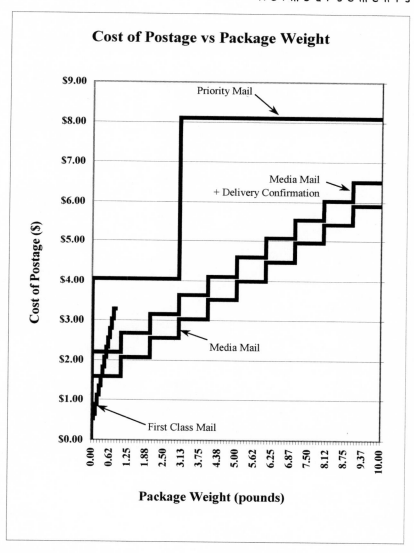

The graph above shows the cost for the various methods of shipping your books for those books up to ten pounds in weight. As you can see, it is most economical to send books via First Class Mail® if they weigh 5 ounces or less, and from then on it is most economical to ship via Media Mail® whether you include Delivery Confirmation or not. At no time is it cheaper to ship via Priority Mail®. That said, it is sometimes more practical to send a book via Priority Mail®, particularly if it is a large and valuable book that warrants shipment in a Priority Mail Flat-Rate Box.

## Media Mail®

The US Postal Service quoted delivery time for Media Mail® is 4 - 14 days (Amazon posts 4 - 14 business days for standard delivery). It is almost always the cheapest delivery method and when customers are offered the various delivery options they usually pick Media Mail® for this reason. For shipments of small lightweight books where the customer has chosen Media Mail® delivery it is sometimes more economical to actually ship the book First Class Mail®. This is where having a postal scale at home is helpful because you can weigh these small packages and determine if it will be cheaper to send them First Class Mail®.

## Priority Mail®

This includes both Priority Mail Flat-Rate Envelope and Priority Mail Flat-Rate Box mailing methods. The method I use is always dependent on the size of the book. I will opt to use the envelope if the book will fit comfortably in it because it costs me only half of what the box will cost to ship.

At the same time, there are a few exceptions to my rule. If I am sending an especially valuable book and I want to minimize the risk of it getting damaged, I will opt to sacrifice a little of my profit and send the book in the box, wrapped in bubble wrap.

On occasion, you may find it useful to use your own packing and still ship using Priority Mail®. If you do, you can get Priority Mail® labels from your post office free.

Priority Mail® label.

## First Class Mail®

The only time I use First Class Mail® as a mailing option is when a customer pays for Media Mail® and the packaged book is light enough that First Class Mail® postage is actually cheaper that Media Mail®.

## Global Priority

This is used when an international customer pays a priority-mailing rate. Think of it as the equivalent of a domestic customer paying for a priority shipment instead of Media Mail®.

If you are going to market your books internationally, there are a couple other things you should keep in mind.

1) Global Priority is not available to all countries.

2) Delivery Confirmation is not available for international deliveries and all means of tracking a shipment overseas are expensive, so there is an inherent risk that international customers will never get their book and you will be refunding them. With hundreds of books sold internationally, I have only had to refund one customer.

3) Fixed marketplace reimbursements are often not adequate for international shipments and any additional shipping costs will come out of your book profit.

There are two sizes of Global Priority Mail envelopes, but I have never sent a book internationally that would fit in the smaller envelope.

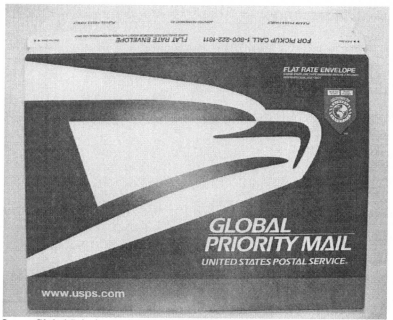

Large Global Priority Mail envelope. This is the same size as the U.S. Flat Rate Priority Mail envelope and books can be packed in the same manner.

You also need to make sure Global Priority mail is available to the destination country as it is not available to all countries.

When shipping books internationally or to an APO address (an overseas US military base) you will also need to fill out a Customs Declaration form and attach it to your shipping envelope.

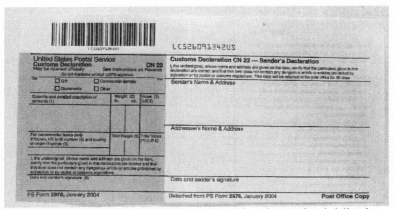

Customs Declaration form. Complete and attach to international deliveries and APO addresses.

## Air Mail Letter Post

This option is used for many of the orders going to Canada instead of Global Priority because it is generally cheaper. You should weigh your shipments to Canada and determine which option is cheaper before packaging.

If you are sending an international delivery via Air Mail Letter Post, you can affix a postal label to the envelope. These labels are free at your post office.

Air Mail label.

## Surface (Economy) Letter Post

Most international shipments are sent by this method and have delivery times of 21 - 36 days. This should be thought of as the Media Mail of international sales. There is a weight limit of 4 pounds to mail a book via Surface (Economy) Letter Post. If the book you are shipping internationally weighs more than 4 pounds, you can still ship it via M-Bag. Please discuss this option with your local post office as it has too many variables for me to include within this book.

In summary, M-Bag mail is a means of delivering media to other countries at a reduced rate, and is intended for minimum weight shipments of 11 pounds. Hence, shipping by M-Bag mail will require that you pay for shipping 11 pounds even if the book weighs only 4 pounds 1 ounce. I recently shipped a book that weighed 4 pounds 13 ounces to Brazil via M-Bag and had to pay $11.15, but the rate varies by destination country. Your post office can supply you with M-Bag tags and information about the cost to ship using this method.

## Shipping Options

There is an array of options you can choose for domestic shipments and only a few available for international deliveries to limited destinations. As is the case with everything else you buy, all of the options are extra. There are a couple of exceptions where you do not need to pay extra for Delivery Confirmation of Priority Mail®, and I will explain this under the Delivery Confirmation description.

## Domestic Mail

## Delivery Confirmation

This option offers a means of tracking a delivery for both you and your customer. It costs $0.60 for Media Mail® deliveries and $0.50 for Priority Mail® deliveries unless you use the US Postal Service Click N Ship® service on the Internet to prepare labels for your Priority Mail® shipping labels. If you do use Click N Ship®, delivery confirmation is free for Priority Mail®, but you will still have to pay $0.60 for Delivery Confirmation on all Media Mail® deliveries unless you subscribe to an online postage service.

Deliver Confirmation form and receipt. This is available from your post office.

Personally, I sell an average of 16 books per day and only put Delivery Confirmation on those that sell for $12.00 or more. I do not subscribe to an online postage service because I do not want the additional hassle of entering address information at this site too. I am willing to risk the loss of the cheaper books, but if you are contemplating running an online bookselling business as a full-time income source, I would strongly encourage you to get an online postage service subscription.

113

I have established a threshold book-selling price at which I automatically opt to pay for Delivery Confirmation. If a book sells for $12.00 or more I will put a Delivery Confirmation on the shipment.

I established this threshold for only one reason. Through all of the online marketplaces the bookseller must give the customer a full refund if the customer claims to have not received the book. This means that a customer could theoretically order and receive a book, and just say they didn't get it for a full refund. If I put a Delivery Confirmation on the book it is a bit tougher for the customer to claim they didn't get a book if in fact they did because there is a US Post Office record of it having been delivered.

I do not want to convey the wrong idea here, I am not saying that you should distrust all of your customers, but the customer pool is in excess of 100,000,000 worldwide and I have opted to establish a threshold to protect my own interests. Delivery Confirmation is nothing more that an insurance of sorts whereby I can see if a book was properly delivered.

## Signature Confirmation

This is nothing more than a Delivery Confirmation plus signature of receipt. I rarely use this and would only consider it for valuable books sent via Media Mail®. The cost of this option is $1.90 for Media Mail® and Priority Mail® unless you use Click N Ship® for Priority Mail® and in this case Signature Confirmation is an additional $1.35.

Signature Confirmation form and receipt. This is available from your post office.

## Insurance

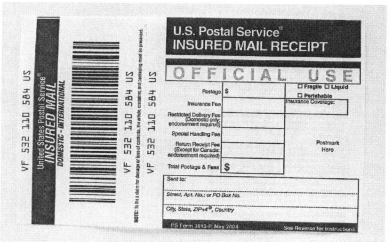

Insure Mail form and receipt. This is available from your post office.
Insurance fees are determined strictly by how much you want to insure the package for as follows (from the US Post Office website):

| Fee | Insurance Coverage |
|---|---|
| $1.35 | $0.01 to $50 |
| $2.30 | $50.01 to $100 |
| $3.35 | $100.01 to $200 |
| $4.40 | $200.01 to $300 |
| $5.45 | $300.01 to $400 |
| $6.50 | $400.01 to $500 |

Please note that I have no control over the changing rates of the US Post Office. I have tried to encompass the most frequently used options and their associated costs, but for a full description of the various options and the current costs of each, please visit the US Postal Service website.

http://www.usps.com

You can sign up for the US Postal Service Click N Ship® service on the Internet by clicking the Click N Ship® hyperlink I have provided (CD-ROM book version) or going to the website:

https://sss-web.usps.com/cns/landing.do

where you can sign up for an account and prepare your own shipping labels.

# Other Online Bookselling Tips And Terms

## Lowball Pricing

Do not allow yourself to get sucked into the lowest price market, you will find yourself going out of business quickly. At the same time, stay on top of your inventory and keep your books competitively priced.

At times you will receive antagonizing emails from other online booksellers, don't waste your time answering them and don't give them a second thought. The purpose of most of these emails is just to rattle you and/or make you second-guess your decisions. I had one seller tell me that I had no apparent concept of book pricing only to learn that he had a book he wanted to sell that was way overpriced and he was trying to get me to raise my price so he could unload his copy.

Do not argue with your customers. The online bookselling policy is that if they are not satisfied they can return the book for a full refund. Tell them you understand their position and that you stand behind this policy. Often a dispute can be resolved by offering a partial refund, if this is a possible solution it may be your best option. It is many times better to give a customer a partial refund than to pay return shipping and have to wait and sell the book again. Remember that giving a customer a full refund and paying for return shipment constitutes an additional investment[15] in the book on your part and it raises the cost and reduces your profit on a future sale.

Keep up your inventory; it affects your fulfillment rate and your efficiency. This is particularly important if you opt to subscribe to multiple online marketplaces.

Do not get sucked into selling books you do not have by using drop-ship warehouses unless you know the drop-shipper will have the book to ship when you need it. Many of the online marketplaces prohibit the practice of using drop-shippers.

If you sell a book that you no longer have, do not try to fill the customer's order by purchasing the book from another bookseller and having it shipped to the customer directly without having an email discussion with your customer. Tell them that you previously sold your copy and that you did not get your inventory updated, but that you are willing to try and locate another copy for them and have it shipped to them directly at the same cost to them. They will appreciate your honesty and may seek you out for their future book orders.

---

[15] If you do not negotiate a partial refund arrangement with your customer, you will be out double the shipping cost (once to send the book to them and once to have it returned to you) and this constitutes your additional investment in the book. The next time you sell it you will need to get this much more for it just to realize the same profit as your first order for the book. So you can see, it might be worth negotiating a partial refund, up to and including twice the shipping charge just to avoid the return.

If you happen to meet another bookseller when you are out buying books, be courteous, but do not pass along all your tips and tricks freely. If you met this bookseller in one of your frequent haunts it is quite likely that anything you disclose will make it even more competitive for you in a direct manner, i.e., if this particular bookseller likes your idea or tip and adopts it, it may very well be used to your detriment.

I have had people walk up to me and ask me all kinds of questions about what I am doing or how I do it. I am always polite, but I tell them that it is a competitive business and it would be detrimental to me to freely discuss how it is done. I even had one lady ask questions under the guise that she had a bunch of books she might be interested in having me sell, but the questions she was asking were obviously questions one would ask if they were trying to get a similar business started. As soon as this was apparent, I gave her my business name and phone number and told her to give me a call if she decided to have me sell her books on a consignment basis.

## Wireless Lookup

There are a few services available that will enable you to look up book selling prices using an Internet enabled cell phone. I am a strong proponent of using one offered by ASellerTool.com. You can get a free 7 day trial by visiting their website and picking a username and giving them an email address where they can send you the account link information and password. If you opt to subscribe to their service, the subscription fee is very reasonable at $4.99 per month. With this subscription they will also give you their re-pricing software to help keep your inventory competitively priced. You can visit their website by following the URL address I provided in Appendix A, or going to http://www.asellertool.com.

They will email other operational information to you after you sign up for the trial of their service.

## Terms

## Fulfillment Ratio

This is a measure of how many orders a particular marketplace placed with you and how many of them you actually filled. If your fulfillment ratio drops below a particular marketplace threshold you will no longer be allowed to list through their service. The purpose of setting fulfillment standards by the various marketplaces is to provide a marketplace venue for reputable dealers to sell and for customers to get the books they order. If you list books you do not have and are unable to fulfill a customer's order, you are wasting everyone's time. The majority of the marketplaces do not want a bunch of middlemen setting up shop and having orders drop shipped, they want sellers that have a real inventory.

## Seller Rating

This is tied to your fulfillment rate on most of the marketplaces and is the marketplace's way of letting customers know if you are a reputable bookseller. It also reflects customer returns, i.e., if a lot of customers return books to you it would suggest that you are saying your books are in much better condition than they really are, and your seller rating will drop. Personally I am not interested in a four star rating if there are five available, and I maintain a five star rating on both Amazon.com and Alibris.com. Abebooks.com does not have a seller rating for customers to see, they use your fulfillment ratio to let customers know.

In the case of Abebooks.com I maintain a 98% fulfillment ration and the only reason it is not 100% is because when I upload many new books I will get some book sales through Amazon.com and within a few minutes – before I can update sales – I get an order for the same book through Abebooks.com. When I reject the second order for the same book on Abebooks.com it counts against my fulfillment ratio.

## Feedback

Some of the online marketplaces have feedback set up for both buyers and sellers. This can be an invaluable tool for future sales. If your customers leave feedback comments that say things like, fast shipment, book was in better shape than advertised, very well packed, seller pays great attention to detail, prompt service, etc., these are things that will influence other potential customers. Do not leave negative feedback for your customers; even if you are right, it looks trite to potential customers.

## Shipping Reimbursement

This is a marketplace term that means how much the marketplace pays you from the shipping fee they collect from the customer. Don't confuse this amount with how much you actually get. Currently, Amazon.com tells you that your account is being credited $3.49 for shipments that are to be delivered via Media Mail®, but you will really only get $2.26 of that reimbursement, the rest, $1.23, is kept by Amazon.com to cover credit card transaction fees and other costs. Don't get too excited about this, on average the $2.26 that you do get will more than cover the actual postage and bubble pack envelope costs.

With US mail postage rates increasing; there will almost certainly be adjustments in the reimbursement payments made to booksellers, but Amazon.com is very slow and reluctant to raise shipping costs to the customer because higher shipping costs tend to slow sales. Besides, Amazon.com is not out anything, they still get their $1.23 after the postal rate increases, and only the booksellers lose.

## E-books

An e-book is an electronic book, one that you read on your computer or using an e-book reader. It is not a paper book, but if you choose you can print it yourself.

## Book On Tape

This is usually a cassette tape that has a recording of a book being read by a professional narrator.

Although I have not done much selling of books on tape, I have recently been adding them to my inventory and have had pretty good results selling them.

Unlike a regular book it is difficult to check out the quality of a book on tape without spending the time to listen to it. At this point, my review is limited to making sure the tape is not broken.

## CD-ROM Books

These are e-books on a CD.

## Large Print

These are special publication runs of a book printed with a larger than normal font intended to make reading them easier for people with reading vision difficulties - like me.

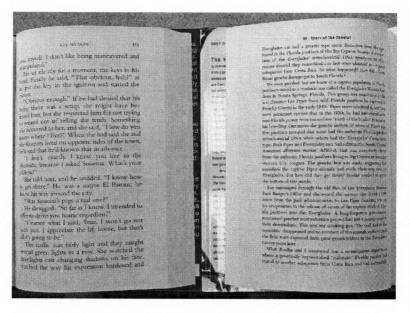

You can see the relative size difference between the large print book on the left and a standard print book on the right.

## Foxing

This is the presence of seemingly random spots, specks, or splotches of discoloration, usually yellow or brownish in color. It is caused by the action of mold on iron salts and usually results from exposure to a high relative humidity.

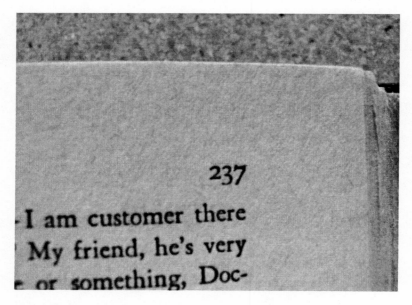

Foxing is the brownish speckles or splotches you see in an otherwise white paper.

## Book Plate

Generally refers to a printed label that has been affixed inside the front cover or first blank page of a book declaring the book is part of a previous owner's collection.

From the Collection of

This is a decorative plate (sticker) that a book owner has put on the first blank page of a book. I airbrushed out the signature of the owner in the photo.

## Chipped

Small tears or chips in the edges of a book's dust jacket.

In this photo I chose a book with some pretty severe chipping of the dust jacket edge.

## Cocked

This term is used to describe a deformation of the book that can be seen when the book is laid flat on its back. In this position, the spine is not vertical and the front and back covers do not align.

The term cocked is used to describe the condition shown above where the back of the book is not at 90 degrees to the covers when the book is put down on its front or back cover. This book is not severely cocked, but it is cocked.

## Cracked

A term used to say that the front and/or rear hinge is starting to break loose from the rest of the book, which will result in a loose cover.

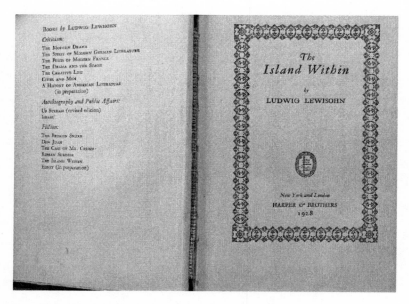

Note how the reinforcement fibers that bind the cover to the spine are exposed owing to the splitting of the paper. This is a severely cracked book, but the binding is still intact. With a little more rough handling, the pages of this book will begin to come loose.

## Inscribed by Owner

This is a way of saying that a previous owner has hand-written words or his/her name in a book. Sometimes the term "Gift Inscription" is also used to declare that a book has words written in it like "Happy Birthday," or "Here is something to read while you are recovering," etc.

## Bumped

Used to state that the corners of a book are bent, usually the result of being dropped, and can include the corners of the pages.

This book has seen some abuse, note how the corners are bumped severely enough that the cover is torn through and the cardboard material making up the "hard" cover is exposed.

## Sunned

When the spine and/or covers have experienced a bleaching owing to exposure to the sun.

Note the dramatic difference in the color of the spine and the cover. The spine has been "sunned," or if you prefer, bleached by the sun. In the paperback version of this book, the "sunned" effect is not very dramatic in this photo. The book cover is a dark orange color and the spine has been sun bleached to a light orange color.

# Websites and Advertising

## Websites

To date I have not established a website (other than the dedicated website for this book) for my online bookselling venture. Not because I don't see a value, but because I have chosen to make this venture a supplemental income business. If I were inclined to do this full-time, there is no doubt that I would set up a website and list my books there as well, allowing customers to make purchase payment through PayPal.com.

Recently I have been considering maintaining a website for my online bookselling business for three reasons in order of importance to me:

1) To provide more information about my bookselling business, who we are, and why a marketplace customer should have confidence in us when placing an order

2) A means of additional advertising

3) To promote this book

If you have the know-how and are planning to make online bookselling a principle income, I think it would be beneficial for you to set up a website to both sell and advertise.

If you do opt to establish your own website, consider setting it up to accept payment through PayPal.com so that you can accept orders for the books you are selling.

If you do opt to set up your own website, and particularly if you intend to set up a customer payment option on your website, be sure to have current virus, adware, and spyware software running on your computer. It would be infuriating to sell a lot of books through your website and find out that your passwords had been intercepted by some spyware and your PayPal account had been drained.

There are a number of adware/spyware software's that are quite effective and free, there are also some that are very good that require you to buy an annual subscription. I personally use Norton Antivirus, Spy Doctor, and Ewido (a free malware program). I had intended to sign up for Bulletproof adware/spyware software, but after paying for their service and waiting several days for the download link, I gave up on them and got a refund. It doesn't matter how good their product is if they can't deliver, so I would only warn you that Bulletproof may be the best, but it is worthless if they don't deliver, and their customer service is outsourced so you can't even get a decent answer to your questions.

## Marketplace Provided Website

This is a great offering by some of the online marketplaces that is included with your listing subscription. You can use this space to tell your customers more about you, the books you are selling, and if you have a specialty that you want to emphasize. Some of these web pages even allow you to post a link to your own website where your customers can get even more information. At the very least you should take advantage of this if it is offered and tell your customers about yourself and your dedication to providing quality books to your customers.

If you plan to specialize in particular types of books, this is a good way to let your customers know. If you are only going to sell collectible mystery series books or cookbooks, you should make a point of letting your customers know so they will come back to you when they are looking for something in your specialty. Also let them know if you are willing to locate a book for them that is not in your inventory.

## Bookmark Advertising

A relatively cheap way to advertise without sending out any advertisement specific mail is to include a free bookmark with each customer ordered book. I am aware of the US Postal Service restriction regarding advertising material in Media Mail®, but I personally do not think this would be construed as advertising material if it is included tastefully. You can have bookmarks printed in most of the nationwide copy store chains and they are relatively inexpensive. It might just help that customer remember you when they are ready to make their next book purchase.

# Legal Structure & Business Plan

## Legal Structure

I am not a lawyer and I do not want my tips or suggestions here to be construed as legal advice or tax consulting advice, I just want to briefly describe the arrangement so you will have a layman's understanding of the scenario. Please spend a little time reading about each of the business legal structures so that you can decide for yourself which structure best suits your needs.

There are several things you need to ask yourself and know before jumping in and starting your online bookselling business.

1) How are you going to structure your business?
   a. Sole Proprietorship
   b. Partnership
   c. Corporation
   d. Limited Liability Company, LLC
2) Where Must You Be Licensed & Registered?
3) State Business License & Tax Registration
4) County Registration
5) Community/City Registration

## Licensing

Many states have a website where you can apply for your business license and each will have descriptions of the structure, legalities, and characteristics of each license. In fact, in many states you can complete the registration of a business name and the business license for a sole proprietorship in a matter of a few minutes and pay for it with a credit card. You might also find that your county and/or city will have websites as well. This can save you considerable time and hassle.

If you intend to operate the business out of your home, but you want to travel to some surrounding cities to participate in street fairs where you will sell books, you may find that licensing in these cities is also required.

## Sole Proprietorship

This is the business legal description for the vast majority of online booksellers and will probably be the case for the majority of you that are considering an online bookselling business.

The scenario for a sole proprietorship - as far as the IRS is concerned - is that there is no difference between the wages you earn in you regular job and the profits you make in your online bookselling business, they are taxed the same. What it will mean to you is that you will either need to file quarterly estimated taxes, or you may opt to have your regular employer withhold more taxes from you earnings to cover the income you are generating in your online bookselling business and the additional tax burden.

As a sole proprietor you will need to file a Schedule C with your annual income taxes. If you have never done a Schedule C before, I would suggest that you have a tax service or tax consultant help you with your first one, or use income tax preparation software. Personally, I have used Turbo Tax since they started in the business and I have never regretted buying their software. Turbo Tax will take you step by step through your entire tax return and prompt you for all of the needed information. The software also has video presentations that will help you along the way and make suggestions for future years that can save you a bundle on your tax liability.

Since Schedule C sorts out the actual profits of your online bookselling business, you will want to keep good records of the business expenses so that they can be deducted from the profits and your actual tax liability gets reduced accordingly. The spreadsheet I have provided with this book will help you with your bookkeeping and sorting of the various expenses associated with your business.

## Partnerships

Just as the name implies, this business is one comprised of two or more partners that may have differing ownership percentages, but each partner is a part owner of the business.

With respect to the business, each partner will generally reap the same percentage of the business profits as his/her ownership percentage. The business as an entity is responsible for filing an annual information return, which is a report of the business profits and/or losses. Once this is done, each of the individual partners is responsible for reporting his/her share of the profits/losses on his/her personal annual tax return.

If you are considering opening a husband and wife online bookselling business and you are considering a partnership, be sure to evaluate whether or not there is any benefit to doing so before getting a partnership license. You may be creating an unnecessary paperwork burden and it will quite likely be a lot easier and carry an equal tax burden to get a sole proprietorship license and put the business in only the husband's or wife's name.

## Corporations

Unless you are planning on starting out big and seeking investors for your business to get started, I would defer filing for corporate status until your online bookselling business is big enough to absorb the cost of setting up and maintaining a corporate license.

In a corporation there are shareholders that have purchased stock in the company; they are the investors that put up the capitol to get started in return for a percentage of ownership. There are specific laws that regulate the issuance of stock and the sale of stock that you will need to understand and adhere to, you cannot just decide to issue stock and do it.

The laws that regulate corporations are quite complex and vary from state to state; hence, if you are considering corporate status, you should involve an attorney to make sure it is formed correctly.

By now you should recognize my comment about having a business that is big enough to absorb the costs of forming and maintaining a corporate status. Just the attorney to consult with about forming a corporation can quickly eat up a year's worth of profit for a small to moderate online bookseller.

At the same time I want you to be aware of the fact that having corporate status can give you access to some additional tax benefits and/or personal liability protection.

## Limited Liability Company, LLC

Forming a limited liability company, LLC, is in vogue and lies between a sole proprietorship and a corporation with respect to both personal owner liability and tax break status.

Like a corporation, I would definitely encourage you to solicit the help of an attorney if you are considering licensing as an LLC.

## Registration

Registration involves the act of filing a company name with the state, county, and/or city where your business will be located and where it will be doing business.

If you are licensing as a sole proprietor, but you do not want your name to appear, you might register the business as, [Your Name] dba [YourOnlineBooksellerBusinessName], where dba is the abbreviation for "doing business as." Then when you set up your accounts with the online marketplace(s) you would use "YourOnlineBooksellerBusinessName." Your business license will still have your name on it as required by most states, but you will be able to use something you register as the name of your business other than your name.

When you look through the books for sale on Amazon.com, you will find all kinds of names for the booksellers that are listing copies of books for sale. The majority are sole proprietorships and the sole proprietors have registered dba names that appear on Amazon.com.

## Business Model, Goals, & Breakeven

This is a step that many new businesses skip over - principally owing to laziness, but if you want to be successful I suggest you take a day or two and plan for success. There are some very inexpensive software packages that will help you develop a business plan, but as a minimum, you should use the business analysis spreadsheet that I have provided to come up with a plan of your own. You cannot drive coast-to-coast and know your path or the waypoints along the way without a map, and you cannot have a destination in your business without a plan.

## Business Model

Once you have determined the legal structure of your business you need to decide if you want a small, medium, or large online bookselling business. In more specific terms, do you want a small supplemental income stream, a substantial supplemental income stream, or do you intend to make this a full-time sole-source income business.

To get a better idea of what you will need for each, I have supplied you with an Excel spreadsheet that you can put your own numbers in to see what might work for you as well as three models I have provided for you to compare to below. Don't worry about inadvertently damaging the spreadsheet, I have protected the cells that should not be changed and left unlocked the ones you can enter numbers in to "tweak" a plan that suits you, and the spreadsheet is the same as the model I have provided here with one additional column for your data. If you do manage to corrupt the spreadsheet you can always extract it from the CD again and start over, but if you fill-in the light gray fields only to estimate your own scenario, you will be fine.

# Business Plan Projection

| | Supplemental Part-Time Income | Moderate Full-Time Income | Professional Online Bookseller Income | Your Estimated Numbers |
|---|---|---|---|---|
| Quantity Of Books Listed: | 2,000 | 6,500 | 8,000 | |
| Quantity Of New Books Listed Each Month: | 165 | 350 | 1,000 | |
| Average Selling Price Of Books (Gross): | $6.00 | $7.25 | $8.75 | |
| Older Listings Sold Each Month (Percentage): | 6.5% | 7.5% | 8.5% | |
| Percentage Of New Listings Sold Each Month: | 28.0% | 35.0% | 40.0% | |
| Quantity Of Books Sold Each Month: | 176.2 | 610.0 | 1080.0 | 0.0 |
| Gross Monthly Sales: | $1,057.20 | $4,422.50 | $9,450.00 | $0.00 |
| Gross Annual Sales: | $12,686.40 | $53,070.00 | $113,400.00 | $0.00 |
| Less 15% Sales Commission: | -$1,902.96 | -$7,960.50 | -$17,010.00 | $0.00 |
| Annual Sales Net: | $10,783.44 | $45,109.50 | $96,390.00 | $0.00 |
| Average Price Paid Per Book: | $1.00 | $1.00 | $1.00 | $0.00 |
| Cost Of Books Sold Annually: | $2,114.40 | $7,320.00 | $12,960.00 | $0.00 |
| Annual Profit (Gross): | $8,669.04 | $37,789.50 | $83,430.00 | $0.00 |
| | | | | |
| Operating Expenses (Monthly) | | | | |
| Phone: | $20.00 | $35.00 | $35.00 | |
| High-Speed Internet Access: | $20.00 | $20.00 | $20.00 | |
| Online Postage Service: | $8.00 | $8.00 | $8.00 | |
| Marketplace Merchant Account Fees: | $39.99 | $39.99 | $39.99 | |
| Office Supplies Expenses: | $10.00 | $15.00 | $35.00 | |
| Car Usage Expenses: | $12.00 | $25.00 | $75.00 | |
| State Sales Tax: * | $57.09 | $238.82 | $510.30 | |
| Business License: | $2.75 | $2.75 | $2.75 | |
| Other Expense: | | | | |
| Other Expense: | | | | |
| Other Expense: | | | | |
| Other Expense: | | | | |
| Other Expense: | | | | |
| Operating Expense (Monthly): | $169.83 | $384.56 | $726.04 | $0.00 |
| Operating Expense (Annually): | $2,037.95 | $4,614.66 | $8,712.48 | $0.00 |
| | | | | |
| Annual Income (Pre-Tax): | $6,631.09 | $33,174.84 | $74,717.52 | $0.00 |
| Minus Monies Spent On New Inventory:** | -$134.40 | -$3,120.00 | -$960.00 | $0.00 |
| Net Annual Cash Flow: | $6,765.49 | $36,294.84 | $75,677.52 | $0.00 |
| Net Monthly Cash Flow: | $563.79 | $3,024.57 | $6,306.46 | $0.00 |

\* Sales tax is calculated by assuming that 6% of your sales will occur in your state and a state sales tax rate of 7.5%.

\*\* Monies Spent On New Inventory is calculated by subtracting the Quantity Books Sold Each Month from the Quantity Of New Books Listed Each Month, then multiplying by the Average Price Paid Per Book, and then multiplying by 12, the number of months in a year, i.e.,:

[Quantity Of New Books Listed Each Month - Quantity Of Books Sold Each Month] x [Average Price Paid Per Book] x 12.

From this spreadsheet I want you to see that the principle source of income is from new listings. You will probably see the same trend in your sales and I can assure you the 28% value that I used is reflective of my own online bookselling experience. Similarly, a value of 6.5% reflects what I have experienced with respect to the percentage of listings older than one month that sell each month on average. You can "tweak" these numbers too, but remember that they are based on five years of online selling experience; they are not guesses or estimates.

Another business figure that you need to know and calculate is your break-even point. This is how much you need to sell each month to realize no profit and no losses. It might seem trivial to calculate and an insignificant amount, but if you never calculate it and don't know what your breakeven point is, you could find yourself starting out too small and six months later finding out you are not making money or even that you are losing money.

Again, I have provided you with a spreadsheet to calculate your break-even point and I have provided additional lines for other expenses you may want to include. I have also filled in the blanks in the first column to represent what I have experienced to be my breakeven so you will have some idea of the considerations I have included in my analysis.

Taking all of this to heart will certainly not hurt you and will give you a much better idea of what sales volumes you will need to run a profitable business, but don't put these tools away after you have played with them, keep them handy and use them to accurately reflect and model your business after you have some real and personal data to enter.

They are dynamic tools and you may find that some of your expenses go up, and when you get better at buying books, some of them may go down. In either case, both your break-even point and your sales analysis model will change too and you should know at any given time what your business breakeven is, and your model will help to keep you on track and guide you to your goals.

# Break-Even Analysis

| | Example | Your Estimated Numbers |
|---|---|---|
| Step 1 - Your Monthly Fixed Costs | | |
| Telephone: | $20.00 | $0.00 |
| Internet Service Provider Charge: | $20.00 | $0.00 |
| Online Postage Service: | $8.00 | $0.00 |
| Marketplace Listing Fees: | $39.99 | $0.00 |
| Total: | $87.99 | $0.00 |
| Step 2 - Cost of Good Sold Estimate | | |
| Estimate by dividing the price you paid for books by the price you sell them for. | | |
| Example: you pay $1.00 for books you buy and you sell them for an average | | |
| price of $6.00, the COGS would be 1/6 = 16.66%. | | |
| | | |
| COGS: | 16.66% | 0.00% |
| Sales Commission Paid To Marketplace: | 15.00% | 0.00% |
| | | |
| Step 3 - Calculate The Break-Even Point | | |
| This is a calculation of the gross sales necessary for you to break-even each month. It is calculated as follows: | | |
| Break-Even Point = Your Monthly Fixed Costs x (1/(1-Sales Commissions Paid To Marketplace + COGS)). In the Example I have given, the numbers used to calculate this are: | | |
| Break Even Point = $87.99 x (1/(1-(15%+16.66%)) | = | $128.75 |
| | | |
| The Break-Even Point for the numbers you entered is | = | $0.00 |

Please note that as you grow your business and incur other costs, e.g., travel to other cities to buy books, preview library book sale admissions, or other expenses, your COGS will increase and you should be aware of the effect of these increased costs by adjusting your monthly fixed costs accordingly. In these calculations I have also assumed that the cost for shipping books and the reimbursements you get are break-even. If you choose to upgrade all of the books you sell to Priority Mail® you need to account for the additional cost here as well.

Again, the spreadsheet is protected and if you will confine your changes to the light gray fields, you will be fine.

# A Day In The Business

Okay, so I have told you about most of the tools and tricks, now I want to take you through a typical day in the online bookselling business so you can have a better understanding of what it is like. I will try not to bore you with such things as brushing my teeth, combing my hair, and other unrelated daily tasks, but I do want to give you a mental picture of what it is like to conduct this type of business and all the facets of it that make up a typical day.

## Morning

Since I sell books online as a supplemental income only, the only thing I do each morning is process and print the customer orders placed during the night so that my wife can pull the books from inventory and package them for shipment. I then spend the day at my regular job.

Last night while I was sleeping, three orders were placed and I can see them from the email notifications sent to me by Amazon.com on my cell phone. Because I list through Amazon.com, Alibris.com, and Abebooks.com, there are mornings where I must log into each marketplace and process orders, but this morning I only need to log into Amazon.com, print the order manifests and shipping information (this information is all printed on one 8-1/2" x 11" piece of paper. I print three copies of each that are used as follows:

Copy 1 -    This copy is folded and put inside the front cover of the book to be sent to the customer, their receipt if you will.

Copy 2 -    From this copy we cut out the shipping label information to attach to the front of the shipping envelope, the remainder of this copy is shredded.

Copy 3 -    This is my copy that I keep for my records. In the lower right corner I write the dollar amount that I got for the book, i.e., the selling price minus the 15% Amazon.com selling commission. I also write the date of the sale and the shipping reimbursement that I received in the sale. The shipping reimbursements will differ depending on the marketplace through which the sale was made and whether the customer chose a standard or expedited delivery. I will later put this information in a spreadsheet where I track the profits of my business and the profits/losses from postage reimbursements vs. postage costs.

I am done for the morning, but that does not mean there is nothing more to do because my wife will clean and pack these books and take them to the post office for the daily shipment along with the books we sold through the day yesterday and packed last night.

## Afternoon

I am off work at 4:00 pm, and today I am going to stop at my local library on my way home from work to see if they have put out any new books that I can buy for my inventory. Since this is my best resource for profitable inventory and it is on my way home from work, I do try to stop here almost every day.

Since I do stop here so frequently, I will not need to spend a lot of time going through all of the shelves because I know which books I have seen and checked here before. I will only be checking books that I recognize as being new to the fundraising shelves. They generally have about 1,500 books on the fundraising shelves, so this never takes too long. As I go through them I am going to post some here in this book, along with an explanation for you as to why I chose to buy the book or not. This will give you at least an introduction into the buy/pass logic that I use when buying books for my inventory.

The information that is boxed is a captured computer image of what I see on my cell phone using ASellerTool.com. I will explain the significance of the information as we go through each of the ten books I am using in my examples.

### Book #1

```
Multi ISBN(Ignore'X') Sep
by Space
┌─────────────────────┐
│                     │
└─────────────────────┘
 ┌───────┐
 │ Fetch │
 └───────┘

1: Book Lover's Guide to the
Internet
Used: .01 .01 .01 (66)
New: .01 (17)
Rank: 1,380,131
=========
```

The ISBN I typed here is: 0449910709

When I use ASellerTool.com's service, I have the option of displaying various levels of information that is available for an input ISBN. I also have the option of inputting multiple ISBN's simultaneously, but I only ever put in one at a time to avoid misreading information on the small screen of my cell phone.

This screen always comes back with book information and is ready to have you input the next book, which is why there is an empty box under the instructions:

Multi ISBN(Ignore'X')Sep by Space

It is telling me I can input multiple ISBN's separated by a space, and for books with an ISBN ending in "X" I should leave the "X" off the number when entering it.

The first bit of information I request is to tell me the title of the book so that I can verify that I input the correct ISBN, so for the book with an ISBN number of 0449910709, it tells me the ISBN matches a book titled, *Book Lover's Guide to the Internet,* which is exactly what I expected.

The next line of information shows:

Used: .01 .01 .01 (66)

This tells me that the three lowest prices on Amazon.com for this title are priced at a penny each, and the "(66)" indicates there are 66 used copies available on Amazon.com.

The next line of information shows:

New: .01 (17)

This tells me that new copies of this book start at a penny each and there are 17 copies available on Amazon.com.

The last line of information shows:

Rank: 1,380,131

This tells me that the Amazon.com sales rank for this book is 1,380,131, which means it is not a popular seller. Remember, the higher the Amazon.com sales ranking, the longer it is likely to take you to sell a book.

I obviously did not buy this book for resale, there are 66 used copies available and the three lowest priced copies are a penny each, there isn't anything to be made. Firewood!

## Book #2

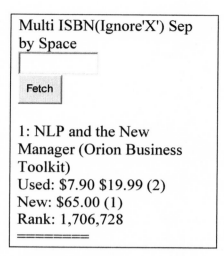

Multi ISBN(Ignore'X') Sep by Space

[Fetch]

1: NLP and the New Manager (Orion Business Toolkit)
Used: $7.90 $19.99 (2)
New: $65.00 (1)
Rank: 1,706,728
=========

The ISBN I typed here is: 0752820761

While this book has a very high (poor) Amazon.com rank, I bought it because it was only $0.25 and I can make about $5.50 on it after paying a sales commission.

## Book #3

Multi ISBN(Ignore'X') Sep by Space

[Fetch]

1: The 33 Ruthless Rules of Local Advertising
Used: $9.52 $10.01 $10.91 (13)
New: $9.50 (29)
Rank: 22,664
=========

The ISBN I typed here is: 09667383, the "X" on the end is left off.

This is a winner at $0.25. With an Amazon.com rank this low, the book will probably sell within a week at $9.65 because it is "Like New."

## Book #4

> ### Multi ISBN(Ignore'X') Sep by Space
>
> [　　　　　　　]
>
> [ Fetch ]
>
> **1: Low-Speed Wind Tunnel Testing**
> Used: $14.80 $27.08 $39.50 (13)
> New:
> Rank: 1,185,028
> =========

The ISBN I typed here is: 0471874027

The book is in excellent shape; I bought it even though the Amazon.com ranking is poor. There are no new copies available on Amazon.com, and there is quite a spread in the prices of the first three books. Based on the condition of this book, I can probably fetch $32.00 within a few months and the book is selling in the library for $1.00. Besides, I am an engineer in aerospace testing and if it doesn't sell I can certainly use it myself.

This attitude goes against one that should be adopted by someone wanting to get into this business as a sole-income source, but since it is supplemental income to me I do pick up occasional books for myself.

## Book #5

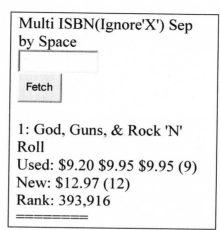

Multi ISBN(Ignore'X') Sep by Space

Fetch

1: God, Guns, & Rock 'N' Roll
Used: $9.20 $9.95 $9.95 (9)
New: $12.97 (12)
Rank: 393,916

The ISBN I typed here is: 0895262797

An excellent staple find! Although the Amazon.com rank is only in the moderately quick selling range, the book is better than very good and will probably sell for $9.85 within a month, making me $6.37 after buying it for a dollar and paying a sales commission.

## Book #6

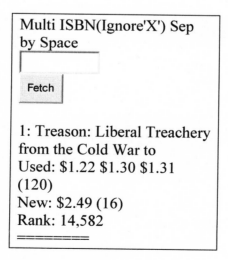

Multi ISBN(Ignore'X') Sep by Space

Fetch

1: Treason: Liberal Treachery from the Cold War to
Used: $1.22 $1.30 $1.31 (120)
New: $2.49 (16)
Rank: 14,582

The ISBN I typed here is: 1400050308

As good as the Amazon.com rank of this book is, the book is selling in the library for a dollar and there is no margin for profit. Firewood!

## Book #7

Multi ISBN(Ignore'X') Sep by Space

Fetch

1: Decision by Objectives
Used: $39.47 $39.50 $43.34 (3)
New: $46.00 (3)
Rank: 240,620
========

The ISBN I typed here is: 9810241437

A real winner! This is what it is all about, the book is only a quarter to me and it is "Like New." I stand to make more than $35.00 profit on this little gem within a month on a $0.25 investment.

## Book #8

Multi ISBN(Ignore'X') Sep by Space

Fetch

1: Truck Stop Rainbows
Used: $5.00 $5.92 $5.95 (18)
New: $15.25 (1)
Rank: 987,000
========

The ISBN I typed here is: 0374240655

This is a toss-up. Earlier when I commented that many booksellers would not buy a book unless it will make them $7.00 to $10.00, this is the type of book I will buy after they leave. Since the book is selling for a dollar at my library, I only stand to make a little over three dollars selling it, but by selling it and a few dozen more like it every month, I pay my subscriptions and the big profit books make me the bucks.

It could take me a couple months to sell this one, but a 325% profit on a dollar over three months investment is respectable to me.

## Book #9

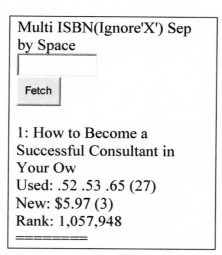

The ISBN I typed here is: 0914629905

Firewood! As much as the title appealed to me as an engineer, there is no money to be made in reselling this book and I passed it up.

## Book #10

The ISBN I typed here is: 1579902367

This is another book I would buy that many would pass up because of the profit margin. The book is selling for a dollar at my library, it is "Like New," and the Amazon.com sales rank is not exactly stellar, but it is a general interest book and I can probably make $5.75 on it after paying a sales commission and a dollar for the book.

I don't want to bore you with too much of this; I just wanted to go through a sampling of a typical book hunt for me at my local library. I went through about 25 other books too, most of which were firewood. The entire ordeal took me about 15 minutes and in all I will probably sell the books I bought for a total profit of about $125.00. That does not mean this stop is worth $500 per hour though, I still need to enter the books in my inventory, clean them, pack them when they sell, update my inventory after the sale, and get them to the post office. It will probably translate to about $40.00 per hour for the time I will invest in this particular buy. Not too bad, a little better than my usual trip, but not nearly as many books as I usually find. The best book of the bunch is shown above, and it will probably fetch a $35.00 profit.

## Evening

After arriving home I will have dinner with my wife before attending to the orders and tasks of the day.

## Order Processing

The first thing I will do each day is process the orders that have come in through the day, and this is done the same as I described for this morning.

## Inventory Update

This is the process of updating my database to reflect the orders I processed this morning and this evening.

To accomplish this I open my book database (I use Homebase, a free software available from Abebooks.com) and I gather up all of my manifest copies from today's sales.

You can download Homebase by going to: http://www.abebooks.com/docs/homebase/main.shtml and then selecting "Free Download" from your Internet browser window.

Using the inventory number that is printed on each manifest, I call up each book individually and enter the price I got for the book in the selling price field. Next I write on the manifest the price I paid for the book, which I read from the database, it was input when I first listed the book. I then change the status of the book from "for sale" to "sold."

This last step is very important because if I forget to change the status before uploading the database changes to the various marketplaces, I will be telling the marketplace that I have changed the price of my book and it will show up as being "for sale" at a lower price. This can and will in many cases result in getting an order for a book I do not have. So, do not forget to change the status from "for sale" to "sold" when you update your database.

After I have input all of the prices for the books sold today and having changed the status of each to sold, I upload the changes to Abebooks.com. With Homebase this is really easy, I just go to:

File + Import/Export + Export/ Send To Abebooks

The program will then open a new screen and ask me if I want to export my entire database or only the changes since my last database update. I will elect to export only the changes since the last update and save by clicking on, "Upload all changes since last load date." And to initiate the creation of a file to upload, I will choose the "Send" button.

The program will then ask me for a name for the file and it will offer a default name. It is probably easiest to let the program assign the default name and select "Send."

Finally, the program will open a new window where I will tell it to connect to Abebooks.com and yet another to actually send the file. After the program has completed the upload, I will select exit.

Now I can close Homebase and backup my database. Any time you elect to exit Homebase, the program will ask you if you really want to end the program and then if you want to send updates to Abebooks.com and finally whether or not you wish to backup the database. Since I choose to use the Import/Export file function to upload changes to Abebooks.com, I do not need to send the updates again and will tell the program to only perform a backup when exiting.

## Updating Spreadsheet

Because I am an engineer and like to work with spreadsheets, I have created one that I use to keep track of my sales. It organizes all of my expenses as well so that filling out my Schedule C is easy. I have included this spreadsheet, "Bookkeeping for Booksellers©" on CD for you to use if you wish, and it can handle up to 12,000 book sales per year.

In it, I record all of the books I sell, the price I got for them, the payment I got for shipping (not the reimbursement), and the price I paid for the book is accounted for in my purchase entries (explained in detailed instructions). I also record the combined postage my wife paid for all the books she shipped today. After all of this is entered I can go to the summary and see how much I have profited on the books I have sold this month. It is a true picture of the business profit because it does include how much I have spent on new inventory, and all of the other expense information I have entered.

## Pulling Stock For Shipment

The next task of the evening is to match the books sold during the day with the customer manifest paperwork I printed earlier. I will pull each sold book from the shelves and insert the paperwork in the front cover for my wife. She will remove all price stickers, erase any prices written inside the covers, and clean the dust jackets and covers of the books before packaging them for shipment.

If the book sold for $12.00 or more I will also prepare a Delivery Confirmation for her to put on the envelope. Similarly, if the book ships by Priority Mail® I will prepare the Click N Ship® label and if the book is an international delivery I will prepare the Customs paperwork.

## Re-Pricing Older Inventory And Listing New Inventory

This is not one of the fun parts of this business, but it is necessary and re-pricing your books to remain competitive will have quite an effect on your bottom line.

A self-imposed rule that I hold myself to is to list at least as many new books each week as I have sold, and keeping up throughout the week means that I do not have to spend the day Saturday or Sunday catching up. I also try to buy as many books I as I sell each week so that I can at least keep my overall inventory quantity constant. This has not been a problem for me, I always seem to have at least 500 books in boxes ready to list and never seem to catch up. If you intend to take your online bookselling to a full-time level, it is not good to have books in boxes that are not listed, you want to keep up all the time and have your entire inventory available for sale.

Anyway, today we sold 23 books, so I will list at least 23 new books and I will review and re-price or confirm that my prices are competitive at least 23 of my older listings that have not sold yet.

So, again using my Homebase database, I enter the ISBN's for my new listings after telling the database that I want to add new listings. Once I have entered the ISBN for a book, Homebase has an "ISBN Lookup" feature that will fill in many of the listing fields, e.g., the title, author, publisher, publication date, and some keywords that help buyers locate books by subject and/or content. Then I copy the ISBN into an open Chambal.com window in my Internet browser and see what the going price is on the various marketplaces. If the ISBN is not recognized by Homebase, I will enter it in Chambal.com and then link to Amazon.com or Alibris.com to copy the listing information into Homebase using Ctrl+C to copy and Ctrl+V to paste.

If all of the marketplaces are similarly priced, I will go to the Amazon.com marketplace to see what books in a similar condition to mine are selling for so that I can establish a selling price that is fair.

I also look at the Amazon.com sales rank to help establish a price. If the book has a low Amazon.com sales rank (indicating it is selling abundantly) I will price my copy higher in the going price range than if it has a high Amazon.com sales rank (which indicates it is a slow selling item). In either case, I usually price my copy above the lowest priced copy, but still low enough that it will appear on the first page of available copies on Amazon.com.

If you price your books high enough that they do not appear on the first page of available copies, chances are that very few customers will even see that you have a copy available until the lower priced copies sell and yours appears on the first page.

The exception I make here is when I have a copy that is in better condition than those on the first page that are only acceptable or good. Then I will still try to price mine mid-range in price with other copies in similar condition.

After I have entered all of my new listing and priced them all accordingly, I will go through my older inventory and do similar research for at least 23 copies and adjust their prices accordingly.

When you are re-pricing, Homebase has another feature that is quite handy. There is a box that you can check that is labeled "for sale" and all of your previously sold books will be filtered out. I say it is handy because before I knew about it I found myself researching for re-pricing and found that I was sometimes looking up books I had already sold. The feature helps you make sure that you are only spending time looking up the ones you have not yet sold.

## Other Re-Pricing Tools

Both Alibris.com and ASellerTool.com will provide you with re-pricing tools as well, but I am an old dog and am quite content using Chambal.com to find out what the going prices are for a particular book.

You should also know and understand that the re-pricing tools offered through the various marketplaces are designed with specific objectives in mind that may differ substantially from your own. That is, what is in the best interest of the marketplace providing the re-pricing tool may not be in your best interest.

This is not the case with either Chambal.com or ASellerTool.com, as neither is in the business of selling books. In that respect, Bookfinder.com is also a neutral website, I just use Chambal.com because they provide me with the going rate at all the top marketplaces that is readily recognized by the logo icons accompanying each price. They also separate the new from the used.

So now, we have completed one day in the business. I do not shop for books every day, but I try to stop at my local library when I can, and that means I usually miss one day during the week and Sunday. I also try to spend one day in the local chain bookstore to browse their clearance shelves and this is usually a Saturday morning.

How many places you need to visit and the frequency of your visits will depend on the availability and quantity of books that suit your specific needs. I don't want to come across as an authority, but I have found even for myself, that finding good books and evaluating their worth is something that is developed, it is not taught, and there are no hard rules. All you can do is get out there, make the best use of what you know and what I have told you, and develop your own skills.

# Bookkeeping and Records

Throughout this section of the book I want you to keep in mind that I am not a tax consultant or a licensed CPA, so I am not telling you how to prepare your taxes or what deductions can/cannot be taken. I am just explaining my understanding of the tax codes and the types of deductions I recognize and take in my own business. You must interpret the codes yourself or have a professional tax advisor assist you with your taxes.

For me to tell you to do this or that with respect to your taxes could be construed as legal advice, tax consulting, and/or accounting advice, and I do not have the licensing credentials to do these functions. However, there is nothing wrong with me telling you how I understand and apply these things in my own business.

Without a doubt this is my least favorite part of the business. Fortunately, my wife does not mind sorting out all the receipts at the end of the year when I need them organized for my taxes because if it were left for me, I would never be ready to file my taxes before the IRS deadline. I would probably have to take my vacation just to sort and organize the paperwork.

I know how to do it, and I know what needs to be done, I am just not very good about keeping it organized. In fact, I have only two files that I keep my receipts in, one for book purchase receipts, and one for postage receipts. Records for all other expenses are on my credit card statements so they are easy to find. I also keep a log in my car for recording mileage on book buying and post office trips.

Despite my shortcomings with respect to the organization of my online bookstore paperwork, my records are very thorough. I am a very firm believer in taking the deductions that are allowed with respect to my taxes and paying only what is required. The one exception is the taking of a deduction for the business use of part of my house; I do not do it and will not do it. I am just not interested in confronting the issues that taking this deduction requires when I sell my home. It just seems to me, to be a way of deferring a tax that is ultimately paid when the residence is sold, and the deferral, complications, and higher rates at the time of sale are just not worth the bother.

I certainly qualify for the deduction; I use about a third of my house strictly for this business, but for my own reasons I just choose not to take it. If you are going to run an online bookstore as a full-time and sole source income, it would probably be to your advantage to take this deduction and I strongly encourage you to keep up with the ever changing IRS tax rules regarding the business use of your home deduction. Rather than provide you with a link to this specific topic on the IRS website; which will quite likely change, I am providing a link to the IRS home page where you can type "business use of home," or "Schedule C" into their search window and be redirected to the topic. You can visit the IRS website and research just about anything with respect to taxes at:

http://www.irs.gov

## Bookkeeping

This isn't really as complicated as it is made out to be. It really only amounts to keeping all of your receipts and keeping good records of your sales. The spreadsheet I have provided you with will help you keep up with them and keep them sorted properly.

There are a number of off-the-shelf software packages that will do an excellent job of recording, sorting, and importing the data into your year-end taxes if you use Turbo Tax.

I personally used QuickBooks Premier (which is overkill for an online bookselling business), but I already had the software for another business venture so I am going to keep using it. [16]

You can even record and track these expenses on an Excel® spreadsheet and transfer the totals to your tax return.

Schedule C has gone through some subtle changes for tax year 2005, and I suggest you become familiar with it by visiting the IRS website and reading both the form and the form instructions. Despite the changes, the key expenses that you want to keep track of and include on your Schedule C are:

## Schedule C; Part I  Income

## Gross receipts or sales (Line 1)

This is the total for which all books sold, not how much you got for the books. Another way to think of it is how much customers paid for all the books you sold throughout the year.

There will be deductions from the sales price you collected later for such things as subscription fees, postage, and commissions, so it is important that when you show your gross sales you include what the online marketplace sells the book for and the postage they get from the customer.

---

[16] This has changed since I released the CD-ROM book version. Because I wanted to provide you with more tools to make online bookselling easier for you, I have developed a spreadsheet that sorts all the incomes and expenses you need to track, and I have started using this myself. Bear in mind that although I use this and am providing it for you to use, I am not a tax consultant, CPA, or attorney, so your use of this spreadsheet is on an "as is" and at your own risk. If you have any doubts, I would suggest that you have your own bookkeeper look over the records of the spreadsheet.

## Returns and allowances (Line 2)

This is the total amount of money you refunded customers for books they purchased and returned. It also includes partial refunds you might have issued after negotiating with a customer.

## Schedule C; Part II  Expenses

### Advertising (Line 8)

This expense includes the monthly subscription fees you pay to the various marketplaces you choose to advertise your books on and the cost of any website you might have to advertise your business. It should only include the monthly cost of the site provider, not fees paid to have someone develop or maintain a website for you. Labor and service expenses are accounted for elsewhere.

### Car and truck expenses  (Line 9)

This is calculated in another part of Schedule C, but relies on the records of mileage you keep for miles driven that are a consequence of your bookselling business.

### Commissions and fees (Line 10)

This is where you will list the marketplace subscription fees you pay and the sales commissions they charge you.

### Depreciation and section 179 expense deduction (not included in Part III) (Line 13)

You may be eligible and choose to take a deduction for your computer, printer, and/or other equipment you purchase strictly for this business. This is where this deduction is taken.

### Insurance (other than health) (Line 15)

If you pay additional premiums for coverage of your online bookselling inventory, the cost of this additional coverage is deductible.

### Legal and professional services (Line 17)

If you paid an attorney to advise you with respect to forming your company, or an accountant to review your records, this is where you will deduct their services.

This is also where you can deduct the cost of tax preparation software.

### Rent or lease (Line 20)

If you lease a storage facility for your book inventory, this is where you will deduct that cost.

## Taxes and licenses (Line 23)

You may be able to deduct state and local sales taxes here if you collected this tax from the buyer and included this amount in the gross sales declaration earlier on line 1. You may also deduct any sales tax you paid in purchasing your inventory

You can also deduct your business license fee here.

## Travel Expenses (Lines 24a and 24b)

If you have travel expenses for trips to other locations incurred in the course of your business, you can deduct them here subject to the limitations as described in the IRS instructions for Schedule C. This might include only a portion of your actual travel expenses if the travel was not strictly for the purpose of doing business.

Sometimes, my wife and I try to combine our book hunting trips with getaway personal trips. When we do this, I keep very careful records of how much time on the trip is dedicated to book-hunting, and how much of it is leisure associated and then distribute the costs accordingly. If you do this too, keep very detailed records, as this is one deduction the IRS scrutinizes closely.

## Schedule C; Part III Cost of Goods Sold

Method(s) used to value closing inventory (Line 33)

In my case, and in the case of most online booksellers, the method chosen is "a Cost."

Inventory at beginning of year (Line 35)

This should be the same as the stated closing inventory for the prior year, but if this is your first tax year to conduct an online bookselling business, it is zero.

## Purchases less costs of items withdrawn for personal use (Ln 36)

This is how much you paid throughout the year for the books you bought for inventory. If you pulled a book from your inventory to keep for yourself, do not include the amount you paid for this book here.

## Materials and Supplies (Line 38)

This is where you deduct the cost of such things as packing tape, stretch and shrink wrap, and self-sealing bubble mailers or other shipping supplies.

## Other costs (line 39)

This is where I list my costs for postage I pay to ship books.

You may be able to take other deductions I have not discussed here so I encourage you to become familiar with Schedule C and to diligently read through the IRS instructions for Schedule C.

If you decide to use TurboTax to do your income tax return, the software will prompt you to enter all of the information in a step-by-step fashion. It will even point out things you might not think of including.

There is one more big deduction you may opt to take, and that is the business use of your home, IRS Form 8829. I want to caution you about taking this deduction. It is a deduction that the IRS scrutinizes and you should document it well. Remember, it could be many years down the road before the IRS gets around to questioning you about this particular deduction, and they do require that the space you are deducting is devoted exclusively to the business. With that in mind, I strongly encourage you to take photographs of the area you use for the business use of your home showing that it is dedicated to the business exclusively.

# Getting A Published Book Listed On Amazon.com

I originally intended this to be the subject of an entirely separate booklet, but decided to include it in this book because some of it is useful to online booksellers that want to list a book that is otherwise not in the Amazon.com database.

One of the most frustrating things about being a self-published author is actually getting your work out on the web for everyone to see and buy. By the time you have completed your work and feel you have something worthwhile accomplished, you find it demoralizing to learn how much it can cost you – the one that did all the work – to let someone else market your work and take a larger portion of the proceeds than you.

When I authored my book, "Online Bookselling: A Practical Guide with Detailed Explanations and Insightful Tips," ISBN 1-59971-487-6, on CD-ROM, I knew there was a market for it and that it would sell, IF I could get it listed on Amazon.com. The trick was not so much actually getting it on Amazon.com, but getting it on there so that people could find it by using keywords in their searches.

Needless to say, it was a frustrating undertaking. The publisher I used to get an ISBN told me that the only way to get it listed on Amazon.com was to enroll in the Amazon.com Advantage program. Doing this would mean paying Amazon.com $30 per year to enroll in the program plus 55% of the book's selling price. This was an unacceptable scenario to me, I did all the work and I was unwilling to give Amazon.com 55% of what I sold my book for, and it seemed a further insult that I would have to pay them $30 a year for the privilege of letting them sell my book and take 55% of the sales price.

The solution was rather simple, but not so easy to find. Amazon.com does not go out of their way to make the solution clear - perhaps because they would prefer that you enroll in their Advantage program so they can sell your book for a 55% sales commission.

If you have written your own book and would like to see it on Amazon.com without paying them to enroll in their Advantage program or giving them 55% of the selling price, you have purchased the right guide.

The first thing you need to do is get an ISBN for your book. There is only one source, or central control, for ISBN's, but you can get one through many publishers, as they are the only businesses that are issued ISBN's. That said, you have the option of becoming a registered publisher and purchasing a block of ISBN's, or, and it is much easier and probably a lot cheaper, you can just buy just one ISBN from a publisher. I used Aardvark Publishing Company (http://www.ISBN4Authors.com) as they seemed to cater to authors and their website made it real easy to both obtain an ISBN and corresponding bar code. They even provide you with the forms for copyright filing.

After obtaining an ISBN for your work, it takes about a week for the information about your book that is associated with the ISBN to migrate to the registry of books in print, but there is no reason to wait to get started on Amazon.com.

The next step is to become an Amazon.com Pro Merchant. This will cost you $39.99 per month, but Amazon.com will give you an introductory rate that is only half price for the first two months. This is where you become the seller of your own book. As with any other book sold through Amazon.com, they will take a 15% commission on the sale of every book they sell, but that sure beats 55%. I have included graphs on the following pages that show you where your $39.99 per month Pro Merchant account becomes an advantage over the Amazon.com Advantage program for books selling for $10, $20, $30, & $40 per copy.

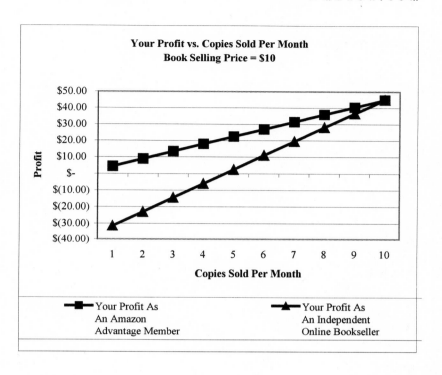

Your Profit vs. Copies Sold Per Month
Book Selling Price = $10

| Book Price | Copies Sold Per Month | Your Profit As An Amazon Advantage Member | Your Profit As An Independent Online Bookseller |
|---|---|---|---|
| 10 | 1 | $ 2.00 | $ (31.45) |
| 10 | 2 | $ 6.50 | $ (22.95) |
| 10 | 3 | $ 11.00 | $ (14.45) |
| 10 | 4 | $ 15.50 | $ (5.95) |
| 10 | 5 | $ 20.00 | $ 2.55 |
| 10 | 6 | $ 24.50 | $ 11.05 |
| 10 | 7 | $ 29.00 | $ 19.55 |
| 10 | 8 | $ 33.50 | $ 28.05 |
| 10 | 9 | $ 38.00 | $ 36.55 |
| 10 | 10 | $ 42.50 | $ 45.05 |

From this first plot and table, you can see that it is to your advantage to be an independent bookseller if you are selling your book for $10 per copy and you anticipate selling more than 10 copies per month.

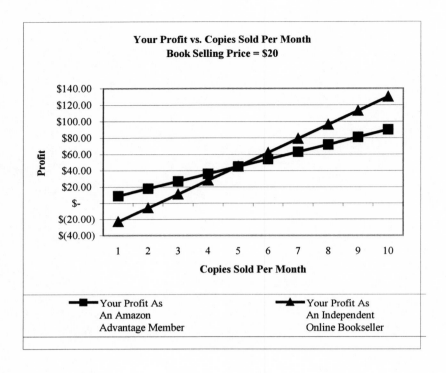

| Book Price | Copies Sold Per Month | Your Profit As An Amazon Advantage Member | Your Profit As An Independent Online Bookseller |
|---|---|---|---|
| 20 | 1 | $ 6.50 | $ (22.95) |
| 20 | 2 | $ 15.50 | $ (5.95) |
| 20 | 3 | $ 24.50 | $ 11.05 |
| 20 | 4 | $ 33.50 | $ 28.05 |
| 20 | 5 | $ 42.50 | $ 45.05 |
| 20 | 6 | $ 51.50 | $ 62.05 |
| 20 | 7 | $ 60.50 | $ 79.05 |
| 20 | 8 | $ 69.50 | $ 96.05 |
| 20 | 9 | $ 78.50 | $ 113.05 |
| 20 | 10 | $ 87.50 | $ 130.05 |

From this second plot and table, you can see that it is to your advantage to be an independent bookseller if you are selling your book for $20 per copy and you anticipate selling more than 5 copies per month.

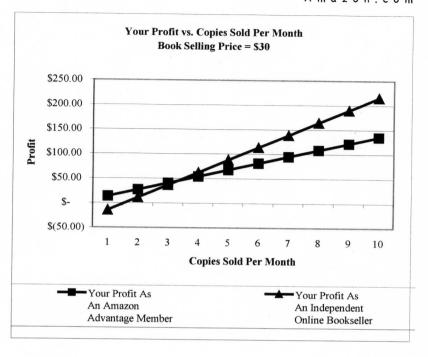

Your Profit vs. Copies Sold Per Month
Book Selling Price = $30

| Book Price | Copies Sold Per Month | Your Profit As An Amazon Advantage Member | Your Profit As An Independent Online Bookseller |
|---|---|---|---|
| 30 | 1 | $ 11.00 | $ (14.45) |
| 30 | 2 | $ 24.50 | $ 11.05 |
| 30 | 3 | $ 38.00 | $ 36.55 |
| 30 | 4 | $ 51.50 | $ 62.05 |
| 30 | 5 | $ 65.00 | $ 87.55 |
| 30 | 6 | $ 78.50 | $ 113.05 |
| 30 | 7 | $ 92.00 | $ 138.55 |
| 30 | 8 | $ 105.50 | $ 164.05 |
| 30 | 9 | $ 119.00 | $ 189.55 |
| 30 | 10 | $ 132.50 | $ 215.05 |

From this third plot and table, you can see that it is to your advantage to be an independent bookseller if you are selling your book for $30 per copy and you anticipate selling 4 or more copies per month.

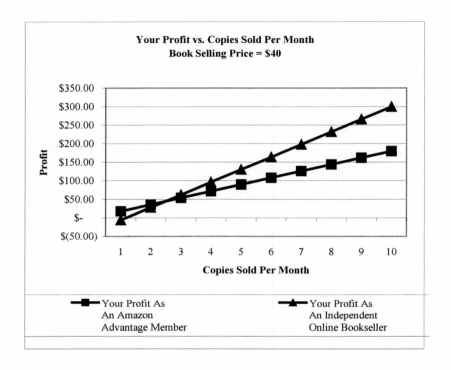

| Book Price | Copies Sold Per Month | Your Profit As An Amazon Advantage Member | Your Profit As An Independent Online Bookseller |
|---|---|---|---|
| 40 | 1 | $ 15.50 | $ (5.95) |
| 40 | 2 | $ 33.50 | $ 28.05 |
| 40 | 3 | $ 51.50 | $ 62.05 |
| 40 | 4 | $ 69.50 | $ 96.05 |
| 40 | 5 | $ 87.50 | $ 130.05 |
| 40 | 6 | $ 105.50 | $ 164.05 |
| 40 | 7 | $ 123.50 | $ 198.05 |
| 40 | 8 | $ 141.50 | $ 232.05 |
| 40 | 9 | $ 159.50 | $ 266.05 |
| 40 | 10 | $ 177.50 | $ 300.05 |

From this fourth plot and table, you can see that it is to your advantage to be an independent bookseller if you are selling your book for $30 per copy and you anticipate selling 3 or more copies per month.

From the charts on the previous few pages, you can see that the higher the price of your book, the quicker it becomes your advantage to be an independent online bookseller rather than to use the Amazon Advantage program. It is also very clear that even if you are selling your book for $10 per copy, you do not have to sell very many per month to make becoming an independent bookseller worthwhile.

Being an Amazon.com Pro Merchant will allow you to do more than just get your book listed in their marketplace, it will allow you to sell other things as well, but unless you know a bookseller that will list and sell your book, you will need an account yourself.

It is very easy to become a Pro Merchant, all you have to do is sign up and pay the subscription fee, but now comes the part that is somewhat cryptic on the Amazon.com website, i.e., the listing of an item that is not in the Amazon.com database and making it so that potential buyers can find it.

It would seem that getting an ISBN for your book and getting it in the registry would be enough to make it visible on Amazon.com and all of the other online bookselling marketplaces, and if you are willing to wait several months to perhaps a year it might indeed get migrated into their systems, but if you want it to happen quickly (two to three weeks) this is the only way I know to make it happen.

With your Amazon.com Pro Merchant account, go to your seller account after logging in. Then on the right side of the screen about halfway down you will find a hyperlink that says, "Create a Product Detail Page." This will take you to an Amazon.com product detail page creation menu, just follow the instructions and enter all of the relevant information that you can, including keywords that will make finding your product, i.e., book, easy for Amazon customers to find.

The next step is as important as creating a detail page for your book where customers can read all about it. JOIN THE AMAZON CONNECT PROGRAM. This is a program offered to authors where customers can read more about you and get notifications of your Amazon posts. This is free for authors and only requires that you provide Amazon with the publisher's name, address, and phone number so they can get a third-party verification that you are indeed the author of this particular book.

I will leave it to you to decide what kinds of things to post as the author of the book. You can look at my CD-ROM book and see what I have posted there, and you can look at the Amazon page for this book as well. Linking to other referenced books for sale on either of my book pages will no doubt lead you to the pages of other books on this subject and some of the book authors are also members of the Amazon Connect program.

The one thing I would caution you about is, DO NOT say anything negative about the work of another author that has written a book on a similar topic. You can see that I have written reviews of:

*The Home-based Bookstore: Start Your Own Business Selling Used Books on Amazon, Ebay or Your Own Web Site* (Paperback) by Steve Weber

And

*Selling Used Books Online: The Complete Guide to Bookselling at Amazon's Marketplace and Other Online Sites* (Paperback) by Stephen Windwalker

If you read my reviews of these books, you will see that I have not written anything negative about either work. I do own copies of both and think that both Steve Weber and Stephen Windwalker have done a very good job of writing their books. It is natural for every author to think his/her work is better than that of anyone else, but if you post anything negative about another author's work, it will look bad to customers and it will sound spiteful.

# Appendix A
## Online Postage Services

Included in this Appendix is a listing of various online shipping services as referenced by the United States Postal Service. I made each a hyperlink so you can visit their websites and get their current subscription rates and services offered.

## Endicia.com

Envelope Manager Software
247 High Street
Palo Alto, CA 94301-1041

Phone: (650) 321-2640
Fax: (650) 321-0356
URL: http://www.endicia.com

## FP Mailing Solutions

140 N. Mitchell Ct.
Addison, IL  60101

Phone: (800) 341-6052
URL: http://www.fpmymail.com/

## Hasler

Hasler, Inc.
19 Forest Parkway
Shelton, CT 06484

Phone: (203) 926-1087
Toll Free: (800) 995-2035
Fax: (203) 929-6084
URL: http://www.haslerinc.com/

## Neopost

Neopost USA
30955 Huntwood Ave.
Hayward, CA. 94544
Phone: (800) 624-7892
URL: http://www.neopostinc.com/

## PitneyWorks

Pitney Bowes, Inc.
World Headquarters
1 Elmcroft Road
Stamford, CT  06926-0700

Phone: (203) 356-5000
URL: http://www.pb.com/cgi-bin/pb.dll/jsp/Home.do

## Stamps.com

Stamps.com
12959 Coral Tree Place
Los Angeles, CA 90066-7020
URL: http://www.stamps.com/

## USPS Click N Ship ®

This is a service of the United States Postal Service and is available online.  Great for Priority Mail® packages.

URL: https://sss-web.usps.com/cns/landing.do

## USPS Shipping Assistant

This is freely distributed software of the USPS that allows you to get discounted rates for Delivery Confirmation and other shipping services.

It also provides a means of building a customer address book and email notification of delivery for your customers.

URL: http://www.usps.com/shippingassistant/

# Appendix B
## Inventory Management, Re-pricing Tools, & Lookup Services

Here I would like to provide you with several inventory management services, book re-pricing tools, and lookup services. I do not think it is beneficial for me to detail the services or subscription costs as these vary substantially and change frequently, so I leave it to you to visit these websites and determine which best suits your needs.

## Price Lookup and Pricing Research Tools

The tools in this section are those that can be used with a wireless device such as a cell phone, or a computer (either via wireless Internet or hardwired Internet).

When I am out and about looking for books to buy, I use my Sidekick II and T-Mobile Internet access, but many of these tools I use on my home computer as well.

You should be conscious of the time you spend researching book prices. It is easy to get absorbed in looking them up everywhere you can, but I have found that if I price my books to be competitive on Amazon.com I will do just fine. Of course, marketplaces like Half.com and eBay.com will many times have the same title much cheaper, but many buyers will only go to Amazon.com so even if my price is higher than the other marketplaces I will generally sell it through Amazon.com.

### A Seller Tool

URL: http://www.asellertool.com)

ASellerTool.com is a subscription wireless lookup service that allows you to check book values using a cell phone or other similar Internet connected device. You can also check the going prices for CD's and DVD's by entering their ISBN's.

They also give subscribers a re-pricing tool as a bonus in their subscription. This re-pricing tool is beneficial if you are an Amazon.com bookseller.

Recently, A Seller Tool has been adding more information to their website to help online booksellers better understand the use of scanners for barcode reading and links to other websites where these tools are available.

This is the service I personally use.

### Chambal.com

URL: http://www.chambal.com/

This is my preferred website for looking up books as I enter them into my inventory because Chambal.com allows me to see the going prices on multitudes on online marketplaces and returns an easily identifiable icon for each marketplace. It also gives me the price for both new and used books with hyperlinks to each marketplace listed so I can get there easily if I choose to do more research.

## BookFinder.com

URL: http://www.bookfinder.com

If a book is not found on Chambal.com, I will generally look for it through BookFinder.com next. For some reason, BookFinder.com researches more book selling marketplaces, but it is not my first choice because it does not return the marketplace icons that help me to quickly identify the various marketplaces. At the same time, the icons tend to slow down the Chambal.com website display, so this is something for you to evaluate for yourself.

Although the BookFinder.com search tool does not have an entry field for ISBN's, it is intelligent enough to recognize an ISBN entered in the "Title" field.

## Amazon.com

URL:http://www.amazon.com/exec/obidos/ats-query-page/ref=sv_b_0/102-3690276-3774535?%5Fencoding=UTF8

Alternatively, you can go to: http://www.amazon.com, which will give you a screen similar to the following:

Then select books from the side bar menu (I put an arrow in the screen print for you) and when this page loads, and you will get a page similar to the following:

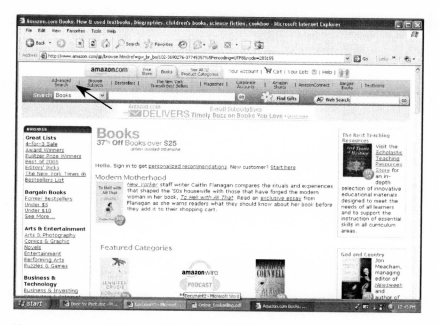

Now you can select Advanced Search (again I have put an arrow in the picture to help you find this) and you will be taken to the Amazon Advanced Search website which looks like the following:

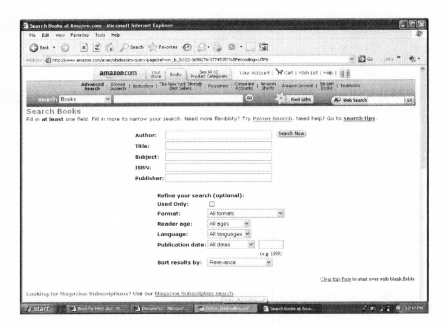

I know these images are not the greatest quality, but they should help you navigate to Amazon.com's Advanced Search web page.

Amazon.com has a search engine for books that are in their database, but it only returns information about Amazon.com sellers, i.e., you are not going to be told how much the book is selling for on other marketplaces.

## AddAll.com

URL: http://www.addall.com/

AddAll.com is very similar to many of the other book search engines, but I believe it searches many more online marketplaces than most. AddAll.com will search over 40 online marketplaces and 20,000 booksellers for both new and used prices. You can search using many parameters, e.g., title, author, ISBN, etc.

## ScoutPal

URL: http://scoutpal.com/

The ScoutPal service is very similar to that of ASellerTool.com, but you can also check Abebooks.com and PriceGrabber.com for current book, CD, or DVD prices. You can lookup using the ISBN or UPC codes. Many of the online booksellers prefer ScoutPal, but their service is 60% more in terms of cost and I have opted to stick with A Seller Tool because it gives me the information I use for less.

## BookDabbler.com

URL: http://www.bookdabbler.com/

BookDabbler.com has many same features of other lookup services, but also allows you to upload a books wish list. The service is offered in three levels depending on the extent of research capabilities you want, and does cost a little more than others.

## BookScoutPro.com

URL: http://bookscoutpro.com/

Advertised to be the mobile pricing tool for everyone, BookScoutPro.com is a fee based subscription service that allows you to check new and used book prices through Amazon.com, Abebooks.com, and eBay.com.

Their service appears to be very similar to others, but I did not see that it returns an Amazon.com sales rank, a piece of data I like to see.

## BookHero.com

URL: http://www.bookhero.com/index.jsp

BookHero.com is another third-party lookup service that can be used on wireless devices like cell phones, but can also make use of barcode scanners.

## FetchBook.info

URL: http://www.fetchbook.info/

Much like the other pricing research tools, FetchBook.info will search many online marketplaces and return the going price of a book from each.

## Pricing, Re-Pricing, & Inventory Management Tools

Be aware that some of the inventory management and order filling software and services will charge you a subscription fee as well as a percentage of your monthly sales. I personally find it annoying that some want a percentage of monthly sales and would never consider using their service. What these services are all offering is the use of software, and I just don't think that any of them warrant a percentage of monthly sales.

## Homebase

URL for download of software:
http://dogbert.abebooks.com/docs/homebase/main.shtml

This is free software distributed by Advance Book Exchange that is used to manage online bookselling inventory.

If you intend to sell your books exclusively through Amazon.com, you will have to export your Homebase inventory and manipulate it into another order and/or format to upload to Amazon.com.

This is the software I use to manage my inventory and it is very convenient because I can upload it directly to Abebooks.com, and the saved "changes" file can be directly uploaded to Alibris.com. Since I have an Amazon.com Pro Merchant account as well, Alibris.com uploads the changes and maintains my inventory on Amazon.com as well. In fact, I process my Amazon.com orders through my Alibris.com account.[17]

## Booktrakker.com

URL: http://www.booktrakker.com/

Booktrakker.com is an inventory management software (third-party) that will upload and maintain inventory on Amazon.com, Abebooks.com, Alibris.com, Biblio.com, Choosebooks.com, TomFolio.com, and UsedBookCentral.com. They are currently advertising that Half.com and eBay.com will soon be added.

## PricePartner

URL:http://www.abebooks.com/docs/HelpCentral/RoboHelp/booksellerhelp/Managing_Your_Books/Managing_books_with_HomeBase/HomeBase_and_PricePartner.htm

PricePartner is the software that is furnished by Abebooks.com to be used with Homebase and re-prices your Homebase inventory. It does not do any lookup; it simply adjusts prices according to the parameters you set.

## Bookrouter.com

URL: http://www.bookrouter.com/

Bookrouter.com is an inventory management software (by subscription) that allows booksellers to maintain their inventory in a single place and have it uploaded to multiple online marketplaces – up to 21. Bookrouter.com automatically reconfigures the data to suit the format requirements of each site and automatically uploads it to each.

They also allow different pricing structure for each online marketplace.

---

[17] As noted earlier, Alibris has implemented a charge of $0.25 for each Amazon order that a bookseller processes through their Alibris account. This is still less than some of the inventory management services and the interface Alibris provides is very user friendly.

Their website currently states that they support the following online marketplaces:

ABAA, ILAB, Abebooks.com, Alibris.com, Amazon.com, AntiQBook.com, A1Books.com, Biblio.com, Bibliopoly.com, Biblion.com, Bibliophile.com, BookAvenue.com, BookSellerSolutions, Books&Collectibles, Choosebooks.com, Chrislands.com, Froogle.com, Half.com, TomFolio.com, UsedBookCentral.com, and Wantedbooks.com.

## Aman For Marketplace Sellers (By Spaceware.com)

URL: http://spaceware.com/product_description.htm

Spaceware advertises their Aman for marketplace sellers as pretty much all-encompassing software for inventory management, order fulfillment, addressing, address checking, etc. To see the product features they offer by going to:

http://spaceware.com/product_features.htm

For my size of business, the software and service offered by Aman is quite expensive, and I have never used their service, but if you have a big enough online marketplace presence, the testimonials for this software indicate it to be a very nice package.

## Seller Engine

URL: http://www.sellerengine.com/

Seller Engine offers a service very similar to AsellerTool.com with respect to both their lookup service and their re-pricing software and is for use by Amazon.com marketplace sellers.

I have not used this service, as it is a bit more expensive than ASellerTool.com, which seems to suit my needs quite well. While I say this, remember than I only maintain an inventory of about 2,500 books and some of the more expensive third-party software solutions may very well suit your needs better.

## BookHound

URL: http://www.bibliopolis.com/cgi-bin/biblio/bookhound

This is a software package distributed by Bibliopolis.com that is oriented to the inventory management of antiquarian and out-of-print books.

Unless you intend to specialize in these types of books, the software is probably not very suitable for you and is quite expensive for the occasional antiquarian and out-of-print book.

## MailExtractor.com

URL: http://www.mailextractor.com/

MailExtractor.com is inventory management and order fulfillment software designed to be used for booksellers marketing on Amazon.com, Half.com, Alibris.com, and eBay.com.

A new version of MailExtractorPlus was just recently released. You can read all about the features of this software if you go to:

http://www.mailextractor.com/whatsnew.htm

## Re-Price Machine

URL: http://www.doolicity.com/

Re-Price Machine, RPM, is software marketed by Doolicity Innovations to assist Amazon.com marketplace sellers with their pricing and to assist with responses to customer email inquiries.

Currently the software is available for a free download and use. You can set your own low price thresholds and margins that you wish to undercut other online booksellers. It seems to me that it is oriented well for lowball pricing, but I have never used it.

## FillZ.com

URL: http://www.fillz.com/

This is another online inventory management and order fulfillment software developed for Amazon.com marketplace booksellers. However, it is geared for sellers with a large volume of sales and has the ability to manage inventory on Alibris.com, Abebooks.com, eBay.com, Half.com, and ValoreBooks.com as well.

You can read all about the software capabilities by clicking on the FillZ.com hyperlink and visiting their website.

## Prager Software

URL: http://www.pragersoftware.com/

Prager offers several software packages for managing inventory, re-pricing, and sales synchronization.

They offer a 30-day free trial of the entire suite of programs and then a licensing arrangement where you can choose the programs you wish to continue using. The prices are reasonable and the features are quite useful to online booksellers. In fact, if I weren't in a comfort zone with Homebase, the Prager software seems to be even more useful.

Similar to BookRouter.com, Prager Software will manage your inventory on multiple marketplaces, but is much more affordably priced for smaller online booksellers.

## BookRepricer.com

URL: http://www.bookrepricer.com/

BookPricer.com is an automated re-pricing tool for Amazon.com Pro Merchants and zshops sellers. There is a monthly user's subscription fee for the service.

## ChannelAdvisor.com

URL: http://www.channeladvisor.com/

ChannelAdvisor.com is principally for eBay.com sellers and auction management.

## BookSKU.com

URL: http://www.booksku.com/

A multi-tasking software for Amazon.com sellers that manages inventory, re-prices listings, catalogues you inventory, manages order fulfillment, etc. You can read the features of this software if you go to:

http://www.booksku.com/features.html

Some features will soon be available for Half.com and eBay.com sellers too.

## SellerMagic.com

URL: http://www.sellermagic.com/

This is another third-party software available for Amazon.com listing services.

## Monsoon

URL: http://www.monsoonworks.com/

Monsoon offers three levels of service options for those booksellers marketing on the seven largest online marketplaces including Amazon.com, but I was unable to determine the other six from their website.

Their suite of software covers just about everything imaginable for an online bookseller, and when I visited their website, they were advertising that the most listings by a single seller using their software was 1,203,823.

Their fee structure is multi-level and in addition to a base subscription fee they charge a percent of your monthly sales.

This particular type of service annoys me to some extent in that I do not see how their service and/or products should command a percentage of monthly sales for an independent bookseller.

## Feedback Assistant & Feedback Forager

URL: http://amazon.wolfire.com/

This is a very handy duo of software packages intended to help you get more Amazon.com feedback by making the task of leaving buyer feedback as simple as replying to an automatically generated email.

You can even tailor the email solicitations to such things as customers that had their books sent via Priority Mail®, or those customers that are geographically close to you and received their books more quickly.

The website currently states that Feedback Assistant is incompatible with Amazon.com's latest website, but that they are working on a fix.

## Readerware

URL: http://www.readerware.com/referaw1.html

If you decide to go to the extent of cataloguing your books, CD's, DVD's, and/or VHS media, this can be handy software.

Personally, I have never bothered to catalog my books because of the time necessary to accomplish it.

# Appendix C
## Wholesale & Remainder Book Distributors

While I do not regularly buy remainder or wholesale books and do not think this information is very useful to the new online bookseller, I wanted to provide you with a list of several sources should you grow your online bookselling business and find yourself wanting to add low margin volume sales to your repertoire.

I do not want to give you a bunch of worthless addresses and telephone numbers here, just a listing of wholesale and remainder booksellers. You can click on any of them and be directed to their website where you can read everything you want to know.

Many of these dealers sell books directly to booksellers at steeply discounted prices, but this does not mean you are going to make a profit buying books and selling them online because while their prices are drastically reduced from the suggested retail prices, in many cases the same books are available from other booksellers online for a fraction of the price you will pay the wholesaler or remainder distributor.

That does not mean you cannot make money buying wholesale or remainder books, it just means you need to research the available titles and selectively pick those that have potential. Remember, there are going to be other online booksellers doing this too, so when your shipment of wholesale or remainder books arrives, don't be surprised if the prices for the titles you bought have dropped. You may find that you have to wait a year or so to get the price you wanted owing to the sheer number of copies that suddenly become available after you placed your order.

In keeping with my intent to reveal all, it would not be fair for me to recommend that a new online bookseller start buying wholesale or remainder books. Wait until you have more experience at determining what sells and what doesn't before you buy fifty copies of a book that will take 200 years to sell.

## A1Overstock

URL: http://www.a1overstock.com/cgi-bin/a1oFront?act=greet

A1Overstock is a source of remainder and overstock books. You can buy books by the skid if you choose. Their sales are wholesale only and you can pick and choose books by category.

## Ambassador Book Service

URL: http://www.absbook.com/

Primarily a supplier to libraries worldwide.

## American Book Company

URL: http://www.americanbookcompany.com/

Principally oriented to test preparation materials and textbooks.

## Baker & Taylor

URL: http://www.btol.com/

Wholesale distributors of books, music, and videos, but is principally oriented to serving schools and libraries.

## Bargain Books Wholesale

URL: http://bargainbookswholesale.com/

Has a large catalog selection of books, mostly remainders or those with minor damage. If you are going to specialize in a particular line of books, they may be worth a visit to see if their catalog has titles to supplement your inventory.

## Blackwell's Book Services

URL: http://www.blackwell.com/

Blackwell's boasts a selection of over 3,000,000 titles and wholesales new titles.

## Book Depot

URL: http://www.bookdepot.com/default.asp?N=0

Has over 5,000,000 titles in stock, mostly remainders and discount books.

## Bookazine Corporation

URL: http://www.bookazine.com/index2.htm

Requires a sign-up to review titles and says the company was formed by mostly booksellers with a knowledge of the business.

## BookCloseouts.com

URL: http://www.bookcloseouts.com/default.asp?N=0

Another wholesaler with a wide variety of catalog subjects.

## BookLiquidator.com

URL: http://www.bookliquidator.com/

A deep discount store with a broad catalog of subjects.

## Books A Million

URL: http://www.booksamillion.com/cat/books

B2B registration is required, but Books A Million has a very large inventory of books covering just about every topic you can imagine.

## BooksNSave

URL: http://www.booksnsave.com/

A small wholesaler with a difficult to follow website. Hit and miss with respect whether or not they have any books available under any specific catalog subject.

## Bradley's Book Clearance

URL: http://www.bradleysbooks.net/wc.dll?main%7Ebd

An easy to navigate website with a broad catalog with books, music, and video titles.

## Daedalus Books

URL: http://www.daedalusbooks.com/

Without a doubt one of the goliaths in wholesale book sales.

## DeVorss and Company

URL: http://www.devorss.com/

Sells only titles of their own publications, advertising metaphysical and spiritual books since 1929.

## East Tennessee Trade Group (Rhinosales by Skuflow)

URL: http://www.skuflow.com/ssl/stores/main/4000000.asp?id=

Originally started out as East Tennessee Trade Group, but now selling wholesale books, discount books, remainders, bargain books, and publisher overstock under RhinoSales.com.

The founder of this company started out with a couple trailers full of remainders, sold them and expanded from there. I personally appreciated his story and the history of the company, and although I have not purchased any books from this company, I will be looking into doing so in the near future.

## Fairmount Books, Inc.

URL: http://www.fairmountbooks.com/default.php

Fairmount advertises being one of North America's largest wholesale distributors of remainder books offering thousands of titles. Like most wholesalers, they have a minimum purchase requirement.

## Fantagraphics

URL: http://www.fantagraphics.com/

Fantagraphics is an adult erotic comic publisher, but will sell wholesale to distributors and retailers.

## Great Jones Books

URL: https://www.greatjonesbooks.com/index.asp

Principally a wholesaler of quality discount remainders of scholarly nature. They have quite a catalog of subjects.

## J R Trading Company

URL: http://www.jrtradingco.com/

They do not keep their inventory online, but you can email them for the latest inventory they have in stock.

## Kudzu Book Traders

URL: http://www.kudzubooks.com/

Registration is required, but this is another goliath in wholesale book sales.

## LRA Books

URL: http://www.lrabooks.com/

A wholesale remainder bookseller.

## Marketing Resource

URL: http://www.mribargains.com/

A wholesale closeout company.

## Maximus Books, LLC

URL: http://www.maximusbooks.com/

A wholesale bookseller that specializes in publisher returns and promotional books.

## MiamiBooks.com

URL: http://miamibooks.com/

Wholesalers of adult oriented materials.

## Reader's World USA, Ltd.

URL: http://www.readersworldwholesale.com/

Registration is required to password access their inventory.

## S & L Sales Company, Inc.

URL: http://www.slsales.com/

A wholesale and remainder bookseller.

## Silver Star Surplus

URL: http://www.silverstarsurplus.com/paperbacks.html

A wholesaler of romance and mystery books by the grab box, i.e., you buy the books by the box as they have packaged them. They advertise that eBay.com sellers do well with their books.

## Strictly By The Book

URL: https://www.strictlybythebook.com/sbtb_web/Welcome.aspx

A wholesale remainder and discount bookseller.

## Sunbelt Publications

URL: http://www.sunbeltpub.com/

Principally wholesalers of regional books covering Southern California and Baja California.

## Tartan Book Sales

URL: http://www.tartanbooks.com/

They sell bestsellers, book club selections, and other award winning titles at wholesale prices.

## The Distributors

URL: http://www.thedistributors.com/

Wholesale book sales to retailers.

## Warehouse Books, Inc.

URL: http://www.warehousebooksinc.com/

This is a wholesale book sales company that sells only to retailers. As an online bookseller you qualify for this, but you must register with them before making a purchase but you can access their catalog and see what they have to offer before registering.

### West Coast Bargain Books

URL: http://www.wcbbooks.com/new/?CFID=1349113&CFTOKEN=24850545
This wholesaler is currently upgrading their website, so I could not address their current offerings.

## WGP Distribution Company, Inc.

URL: http://www.wgpbooks.com/

This is a remainder wholesaler of books advertising 80 to 90 percent off retail prices.

## World Publications, Inc.

URL: http://www.wrldpub.net/

World Publications, Inc., advertises to be one of the largest remainder and bargain book sales companies in the world.

# Appendix D
## Suppliers of Packaging Materials

### Associated Bag Company
http://www.associatedbag.com

### Browncor
http://www.browncor.com

### eSupplyStore
http://www.esupplystore.com

### Fast-Pack
http://www.fast-pack.com

### Gator Pack
http://www.gatorpack.com

### Hillas Packaging, Inc.
http://www.hillas.com

### Office Max
http://www.officemax.com

### Packaging Price
http://www.packagingprice.com

### Pac-n-Seal
http://www.pacnseal.com

### PakOutlet
http://www.pakoutlet.com

### Paper Mart
http://www.papermart.com

### Reliable Office Supplies
http://www.reliable.com

### Staples
http://www.staples.com

### Uline Shipping and Supply Specialists
http://www.uline.com

## Veripack
http://www.veripack.com

## Viking (by Office Depot)
http://www.viking.com

## Walter E. Nelson
http://www.walterenelson.com

# Appendix E
## URL Addresses

I have captured the websites of the references I made throughout the book and listed them here in alphabetical order with their respective URL addresses to make finding them easy for you.

A1books.com
http://a1books.com/cgi-bin/mktFront?act=greet

A1Books.com
http://a1books.com/cgi-bin/mktFront?act=greet

A1Overstock.com
http://www.a1overstock.com/cgi-bin/a1oFront?act=greet

Aardvark Global Publishing Company, L.L.C.
http://www.ISBN4Authors.com

Abebooks Homebase Program Download
http://dogbert.abebooks.com/docs/homebase/main.shtml

Abebooks Seller's Account Information
http://dogbert.abebooks.com/docs/Sell/

Abebooks.com
http://www.abebooks.com/

Addall.com
http://www.addall.com/

Alibris Seller's Account Information
http://sellers.alibris.com/

Alibris.com
http://www.alibris.com/

Aman for Marketplace Sellers
http://spaceware.com/product_description.htm

Amazon Pro Merchant Account Information
http://www.amazon.com/exec/obidos/tg/browse/-/1161232/102-3690276-3774535

Amazon.com
http://www.amazon.com
Ambassador Book Service

http://www.absbook.com/

American Book Company
http://www.americanbookcompany.com/

Antiqbook.com
http://www.antiqbook.com/

Antiquarian Booksellers' Association of America
http://www.abaa.org/cgi-bin/abaa/abaapages/index.html?id=qt6AeZoy

Asellertool.com
http://www.asellertool.com/

Associated Bag Company
http://www.associatedbag.com/Default.asp?cookie%5Ftest=1

Baker & Taylor
http://www.btol.com/

Bargain Books Wholesale
http://bargainbookswholesale.com/

BarnesandNoble.com
http://www.barnesandnoble.com/

Biblio.com
http://www.biblio.com/

Biblion.com
http://www.biblion.com/

Bibliophile.com
http://www.bibliophile.com/

Bibliopoly.com
http://www.bibliopoly.com/

Blackwell's Book Services
http://www.blackwell.com/

Book Depot
http://www.bookdepot.com/default.asp?N=0

BookAvenue.com
http://www.bookavenue.com/

Bookazine Corporation
http://www.bookazine.com/index2.htm

BookCloseouts.com
http://www.bookcloseouts.com/default.asp?N=0

BookDabbler.com
http://www.bookdabbler.com/

Bookfinder.com
http://www.bookfinder.com/

Bookhero.com
http://www.bookhero.com/index.jsp

BookHound by Bibliopolis
http://www.bibliopolis.com/cgi-bin/biblio/bookhound

Bookliquidator.com
http://www.bookliquidator.com/

Bookrepricer.com
http://www.bookrepricer.com/

BookRouter.com
http://www.bookrouter.com/

Books A Million
http://www.booksamillion.com/cat/books

Booksalefinder.com
http://www.booksalefinder.com/

BookScoutPro.com
http://bookscoutpro.com/

Booksku.com
http://www.booksku.com/

BooksnSave.com
http://www.booksnsave.com/

BookTrakker.com
http://www.booktrakker.com/

Bradley's Book Clearance
http://www.bradleysbooks.net/wc.dll?main%7Ebd

Browncor
http://www.browncor.com/

Buy.com
http://www.buy.com/dept/Books_Bestsellers_Online_Bookstore/106.html

Chambal.com
http://www.chambal.com/

ChannelAdvisor.com
http://www.channeladvisor.com/

Choosebooks.com
http://www.choosebooks.com/SESSz16933926611145833613/gr2/en/index.html

Chrislands.com
http://www.chrislands.com/

Costco
http://www.costco.com/

Daedalus Books
http://www.daedalusbooks.com/

DeVorss & Company
http://www.devorss.com/

East Tennessee Trade Company
http://www.rhinosales.com/

eBay.com
http://www.ebay.com/

eCampus.com
http://ecampus.com/

Endicia.com
http://www.endicia.com/default.cfm

eSupply Store
http://www.esupplystore.com/

Fairmount Books
http://www.fairmountbooks.com/default.php

Fantagraphics
http://www.fantagraphics.com/

Fast-Pack
http://www.fast-pack.com/

Feedback Assistant and Feedback Forager
http://amazon.wolfire.com/

FetchBook.info
http://www.fetchbook.info/

FillZ.com
http://www.fillz.com/

FP Mailing Solutions
http://www.fpmymail.com/

Froogle.com
http://froogle.google.com/

Gator Pack
http://www.gatorpack.com/

Great Jones Books
https://www.greatjonesbooks.com/index.asp

Half.com
http://www.half.ebay.com/

Hasler
http://www.haslerinc.com/

Hillas Packaging, Inc.
http://www.hillas.com/

Independent Online Booksellers Association
http://ioba.org/

Internal Revenue Service
http://www.irs.gov/

International League of Antiquarian Booksellers
http://ilab.org/

JR Trading Company
http://www.jrtradingco.com/

Kudzu Books
http://www.kudzubooks.com/

LRA Wholesale Remainders
http://www.lrabooks.com/

MailExtractor.com
http://www.mailextractor.com/

Marketing Resource, Inc.
http://www.mribargains.com/

Maximus Books
http://www.maximusbooks.com/

Miami Books
http://miamibooks.com/

MonsoonWorks.com
http://www.monsoonworks.com/

Neopost
http://www.neopostinc.com/

OfficeMax
http://www.officemax.com/

Online-Bookselling
http://www.online-bookselling.com

Overstock.com
http://www.overstock.com/cgi-
bin/d2.cgi?SEC_IID=13290&PAGE=storelist&sto_id=3

Packaging Price
http://www.packagingprice.com/

Pac-n-Seal
http://www.pacnseal.com/

Pak Outlet
http://www.pakoutlet.com/

Paper Mart
http://www.papermart.com/

PayPal
https://www.paypal.com/

PitneyWorks
http://www.pb.com/cgi-bin/pb.dll/jsp/Home.do

Powells.com
http://powells.com/

Pragersoftware.com
http://www.pragersoftware.com/

Price Partner by Abebooks
http://www.abebooks.com/docs/HelpCentral/RoboHelp/booksellerhelp/Managing_Y
our_Books/Managing_books_with_HomeBase/HomeBase_and_PricePartner.htm

PriceGrabber.com
http://www.pricegrabber.com/

Reader's World Wholesale
http://www.readersworldwholesale.com/

Readerware.com
http://www.readerware.com/referaw1.html

Reliable Office Supplies
http://www.reliable.com/reliable/home.html

Re-Price Machine by Doolicity
http://www.doolicity.com/

S & L Sales Company
http://www.slsales.com/

Sam's Club
http://www.samsclub.com/shopping/navigate.do?dest=0

ScoutPal.com
http://scoutpal.com/

SellerEngine.com
http://www.sellerengine.com/

SellerMagic.com
http://www.sellermagic.com/

Silver Star Surplus
http://www.silverstarsurplus.com/paperbacks.html

Stamps.com
http://www.stamps.com/

Staples
http://www.staples.com/webapp/wcs/stores/servlet/home?storeId=10001&langId=-1&krypto=mfxq1nTSMWh0shUQOLdqejr6zGQ2Y8NL

Strictly by the Book
https://www.strictlybythebook.com/sbtb_web/Welcome.aspx

Sunbelt Publications
http://www.sunbeltpub.com/

Tartan Book Sales
http://www.tartanbooks.com/

Textbookx.com
http://brandselections.com/dir/textbookx.html

The Distributors
http://www.thedistributors.com/

TomFolio.com
http://tomfolio.com/

TurboTax
http://www.turbotax.com/?source=sgbk05&priorityCode=3718052168&cid=ppc_gg
_b_stan_TurboTax

Uline Shipping and Supply Specialists
http://www.uline.com/

United States Postal Service
http://www.usps.com/
UsedBookCentral.com
http://usedbookcentral.com/

USPS Click N Ship
https://sss-web.usps.com/cns/landing.do

USPS Shipping Assistant
http://www.usps.com/shippingassistant/

Veripack
http://www.veripack.com/

Viking (by Office Depot)
http://www.viking.com/

Walmart.com
http://www.walmart.com/

Walter E. Nelson
http://www.walterenelson.com/

Wantedbooks.com
http://www.wantedbooks.com/

Warehouse Books, Inc.
http://www.warehousebooksinc.com/

West Coast Bargain Books
http://www.wcbbooks.com/new/?CFID=1349113&CFTOKEN=24850545

WGP Distribution Company, Inc.
http://www.wgpbooks.com/

World Publications. Inc.
http://www.wrldpub.net/

# Appendix F
## Frequently Asked Questions
### A Compilation of Questions Asked by Customers & Prospective Customers

*"The online bookselling business sounds enticing, but I do not want to be tied down by a business. If I have an online bookselling business, will I need to pay someone to handle my orders and shipments when I go on vacation?"*

The long and the short answers are both no. I do not want to be tied down to a business either, and I would not be an online bookseller if I could not close it at my convenience. All of the online bookselling marketplaces have a "hold" feature for your inventory. Some of them refer to this as putting your inventory on vacation. If you want to close your store for a vacation, all you need to do is give the marketplace(s) a few days notice telling them to make your inventory unavailable for purchase, and all of your books will be taken off their active databases. Doing this is as simple as going to your seller controls and selecting the vacation option and the dates you will be gone. You can even leave the re-opening date undetermined and your books will be put on hold until you return and reactivate your inventory. Both putting your books on hold and having your inventory reactivated can take a couple days, so don't forget to account for this.

*"I have seen a lot of advertisements for book scouts, why would I want to become an online bookseller and sell only some of the books I list when I could be a book scout and get paid for every book I buy and ship to the company I scout for?"*

There are a number of advantages to being an online bookseller yourself and few advantages to scouting for someone else. I will demonstrate the advantages of being an online bookseller yourself below, and sum up the advantages of scouting for someone else here.

As a scout for someone else, you will be paid for every book the service you work for tells you to buy, on the order of 10% to 15% of the real value of the book. Some will even pay you something for shipping the books to their warehouse. That is it, you are assured of a sale for every book they tell you to buy, but the catch is that you will only be paid a fraction of what you could get as an online bookseller yourself.

I personally feel this is a good example of the old saying, "You can't judge a book by its cover." in that it sounds good in the advertising, but a little research will reveal what you will sacrifice and now I will explain.

Suppose you are out scouting for books and run across:

"Kate: The Kate Moss Book," by Kate Moss, ISBN 0789301016, [Paperback]

If you are scouting for a service, you will be told to purchase the book and that you will be paid $30.00 for it in addition to the $1.99 reimbursement for purchasing it. You will not be told the real value of the book, but since I recently sold a copy of it for $199.99, I can say for the sake of simplicity that it is worth $200.00. The $30.00 that you will get for "finding" it represents 15% of the real value, and this is probably generous because most "services" you can scout for will pay you closer to 10% of the real value.

If you were scouting for your own online bookselling business using a wireless lookup service, you would see that the book has a low online value of $190, a high online value of $220.00, and an Amazon.com sales rank of about 100,000, which means that even at this high price, the book is fairly popular. There is no question, you buy the book and put it up for sale online. If like me, you price the book toward the middle of those being offered, you will probably have it in your inventory for a couple months before it sells, at which time you will make a profit of about $168.00 after paying a 15% sales commission to the marketplace it sells through. That is 5.6 times as much as you will get finding it as a scout for someone else, or $138.00 more!

In my case, I only paid $0.90 for the book and realized a profit of $169.09 after paying the marketplace commission, or 18,788%, and I had it in my inventory for about two months.

I don't want to mislead you, this was a gem that I sold, and this kind of sale does not happen every day, but I do have a dozen or so such sales each month and you could too. The difference in 12 such sales each month (for sales comparable to the example above) is $1,656.00 more in your pocket as an independent online bookseller than as someone's scout.

Another thing to consider is the large number of books in the $8.00 to $10.00 range. As a scout you might be instructed to pass on these books because the cost of the book, shipping it to a warehouse, and paying you a commission doesn't leave enough profit to be had by the service you are scouting for. As an independent online bookseller, these same books could make you $5.80 to $7.50 each if you were to pay a dollar for them.

Thus, you can now see and understand why it is to your benefit to be an independent online bookseller and not just a minimum commission scout for someone else. The costs associated with being an independent bookseller are covered by the sale of just a few books each month. The sale of a single "gem" can cover the costs for a few months.

---

*"There are so many different online marketplaces, which one should I list my books on?"*

Personally, I list my books on several, but this means paying multiple monthly subscriptions for listing. If you are just getting started and want to keep your expenses to a minimum, i.e., you have to choose only one; I would suggest Amazon.com for two reasons. First, they are the biggest online marketplace with the most buyers, and second because choosing any other single marketplace will result in fewer sales for you which could be just the discouragement you need to give up, and I want you to be successful.

---

*"Where do I find the Amazon.com sales rank, what does it really mean to me, and is it really significant?"*

The Amazon.com sales rank is found under the "Product Details" of every book listed on Amazon.com. They list the current sales rank as well as the sales rank for the same book yesterday, and it is only a measure of how well that book is selling on Amazon.com. This is a little deceptive because if the book is a Barnes and Noble publication, it might be selling very well on the Barnes and Noble website, but not on the Amazon.com website, so don't view the Amazon.com sales rank as the true popularity of a particular title. My own book sells quite well through my website, with customers choosing to buy it using PayPal direct purchases instead of Amazon.com, so the sales rank of my book is only reflective of how many customers purchase through the Amazon marketplace.

As a buyer, many people refer to the Amazon sales rank as a measure of how popular a book is, and this is fine to do as long as you recognize that it is a measure of buyer popularity on Amazon only. Booksellers on the other hand use the Amazon sales rank as a measure of how quickly they might sell a particular title if they buy it for their inventory. I myself look at the Amazon sales rank, which is returned by the A Seller Tool software I subscribe to, but I do not make a purchase decision based solely on the Amazon sales rank of a book. For more discussion on this, please refer to sections of the book that address the Amazon sales rank.

---

*"I have read on the Internet that some online booksellers will not buy a book unless they can make some threshold profit that they have established for themselves. Should I establish a minimum profit threshold for the inventory I buy?"*

I have an acquaintance that is an online bookseller and he has established a threshold profit margin of $10 for the books he buys to list. I really like running into him when I am out buying books because I concentrate on identifying books that will return higher profits and he hands me all the ones that don't quite meet his threshold. I get a lot of books that he rejects which make me anywhere from $5 to $9, and I get the winners that I focus on while he is looking up these lower profit books for me.

When I am buying books, I am more concerned with making a profit than setting a minimum profit. If I find a small paperback that I can buy for $0.90, sell for $4.75 plus $2.26 in shipping reimbursement, pay $0.71 in online commission and ship for $1.59 plus $0.20 for a standard envelope, and it has an Amazon sales rank that indicates I can sell it within a few weeks, I will buy it and make a profit of $4.32 on it. That is a profit of 480%. To me, setting a threshold profit margin seems a bit contradictory to the concept of making money, but since I only do this part-time, I can understand why a full-time bookseller might want to limit the time he/she spends packing lower profit books. While I do not personally establish a threshold, I do consider many factors for books that show promise of small profit margins, including, the size and weight of the book (can I make anything from the shipping reimbursement), the Amazon sales rank (how long will I have to wait to recover my investment), and the condition of the book itself.

If you are planning to be an online bookseller on a full-time basis, it might be a good idea to evaluate the profit threshold scenario because every book you buy will occupy space, every book you buy will require your time to prepare and ship, and it might be worth your effort to concentrate only on books with higher profit margins. As a part-time bookseller that is selling fewer books and maintaining a smaller inventory, the lower profit books will pay your marketplace subscription fees and the real winners will provide you with the profits that make it worthwhile.

---

*"There are so many cell phones available and different scanners that can be used with each, how do I decide which is best for me?"*

This is a question that there is no single answer to because the services vary across the country and every individual has different preferences.

Personally, I use a Sidekick II phone and T-Mobile service. The phone has good coverage, but it is very awkward to use because when I flip the screen open to reveal the QWERTY keyboard, it takes both thumbs to type, not leaving me with a free hand to hold a book open. I will be investigating a different phone in the near future and possibly a scanner as well.

I think the best way to answer this question is to talk with other people in your particular area that have cell phones with Internet access. Ask them about their coverage and how often they experience problems with Internet access. Then, go down to the various mall stores representing the services that are of interest to you and look at their phones. Make sure you can easily read the screens and conveniently operate the phone one-handed. Quite often a book will not have an ISBN on the back cover, which will require that you open the book to find the ISBN inside. It is difficult to hold a book like this and operate a cell phone with two hands at the same time.

---

*"I have read some of your blogs on the Internet and I would like to know why you don't promote bookselling on eBay."*

Ebay is great for bookselling if you are trying to sell a collection of books by the same author, theme, or bulk lots of books, but very time consuming for individual titles. All of the major online marketplaces provide cover images for most books, as well as the other information if you supply an ISBN, but to sell on eBay, you have to provide all the information for each auction, set up individual auctions for each book, and pay listing fees for each auction whether the book sells or not.

I am sure eBay will make changes in the future to accommodate online bookselling, but at this time it is just too time consuming to sell individual books through them.

---

*"Do you use or recommend using a cell phone and scanner at book sales?"*

I have personally never used a scanner at a book sale, but will probably add one to my toolbox in the near future.

The reason I have never used one stems from watching my son at a large book sale and seeing how many more books he left with than the booksellers that were scanning every title before buying. It was a small university book sale with about 40,000 titles being sold. I watched my son looking over the titles and pulling the ones he instinctively felt were winners, many times from the same tables as other booksellers using scanners. When all was said and done, he had purchased about 325 books and paid $325 for them. I did not see another bookseller leave with more than 75 titles. After my son listed all but the losers (43 he called losers, and a loser to my son is any book that will not make him a profit of $15), he recovered his investment within 24 hours and within a week he profited over $5,000 from those he did list.

My own experience with book sales has not been quite this profitable, but I do know that if I waste the time checking every book with a scanner I am going to have many winners snatched up from right in front of me by other booksellers, so I do not even bother taking my cell phone with me to a book sale.

That said, I would stick to the practice that has served me well, but modify it to profit me more. I do intend to add a scanner to my toolbox soon, and I will use it at book sales, but only for the second and third sweeps of available titles. That is, I will still go through the available books quickly, identify and box up all the ones I instinctively feel are winners, and then after the frenzy has died down a little, I will take my time and go through others that I think may be good and spend some time scanning them.

Book sales, particularly preview sales, are just to fast paced to spend time scanning books. You have to have some knowledge of what sells online and grab them up quickly or another online bookseller will beat you to it. The books are also relatively cheap, so the winners you are able to get far outweigh the losers. Sure, it would be better to leave with only winners, but that is not practical given the atmosphere and nature of the online bookselling business. I would much rather leave with 200 books, 150 winners and 50 losers, that will make me a profit of $3,000 than leave with only 50 winners that will make me a profit of only $1,000.

---

*"When your book first came out on CD-ROM, you said you did not have any plans to put it in a paperback form. Why have you decided to publish it in paperback?"*

I didn't have any plans to publish this book in paperback, but many prospective customers were insistent that I put it out in paperback for many different reasons.

I still think the CD-ROM book is more useful and efficient because it gives the reader almost instant access to the myriad of websites I refer to in the book. With the paperback, the reader must first find this book, then look up the referenced website URL, then start their computer, open their browser, and then type in the

URL. With the CD-ROM book stored on their computer, it isn't even necessary to look for the book and there is no typing, only mouse clicking.

Anyway, I do not want to impose what I think is efficient or convenient on my customers, so I converted the book to a format suitable for paper publishing and put it out in paperback.

I believe the reason most customers wanted it in paperback was they wanted to be able to read it anywhere and not be tied to their computer. I can understand that and I myself have many reference books for online bookselling that are in paperback form. Personally I do not like to read books on my computer either.

---

*"I have been selling books online for a couple years and wanted to know your thoughts about how to handle orders that are received for books you have already sold and were not removed from your inventory for whatever reason."*

It is inevitable that you will sell a book you don't have for one reason or another. This usually happens to me when I sell a book through one marketplace and do not get my inventory updated on another marketplace quickly enough.

What I usually do is contact the customer that placed the second order for the book and ask them if they would like for me to locate another copy for them, but only after I have checked to see if another copy is available from an online bookseller with a good reputation. I also offer to have it shipped to them for the same price they intended to purchase it from me, but I make them aware of the fact that it is going to be drop-shipped to them from another bookseller.

If there are no other copies available, or if the customer tells me they do not want to have a book drop-shipped from another bookseller, I simply apologize for having the book listed after it has already sold elsewhere and I refund them the full amount of their purchase and shipping charges.

This is certainly one of the drawbacks of listing through multiple marketplaces that do not have linked databases, and one of the reasons I have considered many time to sell through only Amazon.

---

*"I am just getting ready to start an online bookselling business and I have decided to sell through Amazon.com only, but I don't know if I should subscribe for a Pro Merchant account or just list through them and pay $1.00 per book in sales, can you explain the differences to me?"*

As you mentioned, there are two ways to sell books through Amazon.com's marketplace. The easy way to decide which is best for you is to first recognize that both will charge you a 15% sales commission and pay you the same shipping reimbursements. So, the only real difference is to determine if you want to pay $40 per month for a Pro Merchant account or $1.00 per book sold for a standard account. To make the decision really requires some forecasting on your part. If you expect to sell more than 40 books a month, it is more economical to have a Pro Merchant account, if not, then it would be better to have a standard seller's account.

Consider the total number of books in your inventory that you will be listing online and come up with a percentage of books that will sell each month that you are comfortable with. For example, I have about 3,000 books in my inventory and each month I add about 400 books. From experience I have pound that about 35% of my new listing each month will sell, so approximately 140 of my new listings will sell. I have also found that 7.5% of my old listings will sell each month, or about 225 books. Thus, I sell about 365 books each month.

If you are starting out with 100 books and plan to initially add 100 books each month, your first month you will sell about 35 of your original inventory and some percentage of the 100 you are adding which will depend on how early in the month you add them, but lets say you don't sell any of the new listings the first month. There would seem to be a $5 advantage for you to sell the first month with only a standard account, and after that, to have a Pro Merchant account, but that is not the case because Amazon.com will give you a Pro Merchant account for $19.99 per month for the first two months.

I believe that if you have at least 60 books to get started, and you intend to initially add to your inventory very quickly, i.e., 100 books per month for a while, it will definitely be to your advantage to get a Pro Merchant account right away.

---

*"I have seen a number of advertisements for resale rights to ebooks, what is your experience with them?"*

I have a few ebooks listed for sale, including my own on CD, but other than my own book, I have found them to be a waste of time. If you have to buy them to get the resale rights, it is also a waste of money. Like large lots of books available on eBay, there are a lot of auctions for ebooks and some offering hundreds of titles with resale rights. I have never bought any of these ebooks or resale rights, but I have found some free resources for ebooks that are works whose copyright has expired. I have converted a few to ebooks that I could put on CD and sell, but they are not very popular and most are nothing more than a waste of time to convert and list.

If the ebooks being sold on eBay were the great sellers that the people auctioning them for would have you believe, they wouldn't be selling them with resale rights for $3.99, they would be marketing them to customers and selling them directly for the profits they claim you could make. You can't even burn them as firewood because they have no value.

---

*"I have been looking at some of the auctions for bulk lots of books at wholesale prices being offered on eBay, do you have any advice for me about them?"*

Yes, beware! Many of the bulk lots offered on eBay as unsorted lots are bogus; they are the firewood from another bookseller's inventory that he/she is trying to dump on a beginner. If an auction sounds good, ask the seller to provide you with a list of the titles in the auction, or more photographs that show the book titles so you can do some research. If they won't send you this information, stay away. You can also look at the seller's feedback to see if they have sold similar lots in previous auctions. Negative feedback would certainly indicate a less than honest seller.

I don't want to say that all such auctions are bogus because I know some are legitimate. I am personally aware of one seller that is actually a rather large company. They work with a Bankruptcy Trustee and auction off the estates of both individuals and companies in bankruptcy. While I have not seen them auction any large lots of books, if they did and claimed the lot to be unsorted, I would know they are running a legitimate auction as they do not have the time or interest to hand-pick the books to sell the winners online.

Use a healthy dose of skepticism when you are looking at online auctions of book lots.

---

*"Can I sell books on Amazon.com that do not have an ISBN?"*

Yes, but it takes a bit more effort to get it listed on Amazon. The first thing to do would be to perform an advanced search on the Amazon website using the title and/or author, (http://www.amazon.com/exec/obidos/ats-query-page/103-1185506-4708616) to see if they have assigned an ASIN, Amazon Standard Identification Number, to identify this particular book because many pre early 1970's books do not have an ISBN and they still list and sell on Amazon. If you find an ASIN for this book, you can use it to sell your copy, if not, there is still a way to list it on Amazon if, and only if, you are a Pro Merchant. This other way involves creating a product detail page.

Regardless, do some research to see what the value of the book is before you establish a price for your copy. I would recommend Chambal and Bookfinder as both search many marketplaces to see if other copies are available. You don't want to sell your copy too cheap, especially if you have to put more time into getting it listed.

---

*"I have a rather large collection of books myself and I am interested in online bookselling, but I don't know if I should get into it to sell my books myself or take them down to a local chain bookstore and sell them there, do you have any suggestions?"*

There are trade-offs you must consider and evaluate yourself.

If you take your books down to sell at a local bookstore, you will not be getting a fair market value for them. In fact, I shop at a large chain bookstore regularly and see people bring in boxes of books. When I am looking through the clearance shelves I can even see the titles they are selling and know they are being offered about 10% - 15% of the online value for their books. Thus, if the bookstore is willing to pay $45.00 for a couple boxes of books, you can be sure they are worth between $200 and $300 to the bookstore, and perhaps considerably more online.

The down side to selling them yourself online is that you will have to set up a marketplace account and list them for sale. Then you will need to clean, pack and ship them when they sell. If you aren't in a hurry to sell them, these inconveniences could bring you a lot more money for your books.

Finally, if you are considering online bookselling beyond your own collection, there are definite advantages to having your own large collection to start with because you don't need to wait until you can find some books for an initial inventory.

In summary, it is a question of whether or not you want to go to the effort and trouble of selling individual titles yourself, or whether you would rather just clear out your collection and accept 10% - 15% of their worth by selling to a bookstore.

---

*"I have purchased and read other books about online bookselling that recommend and promote wholesale and remainder books. In fact, many of these other books really hype the fact that they have exclusive lists of wholesale and reminder book distributors. How do you feel about selling wholesale and remainder books?"*

First, I want to set the record straight. I too provide an "exhaustive" list of wholesale and remainder book distributors, but I feel like the authors that promote their books based on exclusive lists are being deceptive. There is nothing exclusive about their lists; in fact, an Internet search for wholesale and remainder books will yield almost all of these distributors.

Next, I would like to discuss the entire concept of buying wholesale and remainder books to sell online. It can be an expansive learning experience for the beginner. Books are not made available as remainders because the distributors feel like having online booksellers make some money on sales, they are made remainders because the publishers have reached a point where they feel the market is saturated with a particular title and they have remaining stock. Wholesale books are not much different except that they quite often cost more than remainders.

If there is any real money to be made selling the titles available from these wholesale and remainder book distributors, they would not be making them available for online booksellers, they would be selling them to the customers themselves.

All that said, you can make money buying wholesale and remainder books if you do your research and you are very selective about the titles you buy. The profit margins will probably be lower since the market has been oversupplied, but over time you can make money.

I personally bought quite a few books from Webster Wholesale Books before they went out of business, and I did make some money on the overall purchase, but I was lucky and able to buy some titles that were still in moderate demand.

Just be careful when buying from wholesale and remainder book distributors. Do some research of the titles available for both price and demand. I have found that many titles being sold by remainder book distributors are already available, new, on Amazon for pennies, and the distributor still wants several dollars per copy.

---

*"I am considering online bookselling as a second income source, but I don't have money to waste and would like to know what the realistic cost of getting started would be before I even buy your book about it. I have bought other "opportunity" books before and found them to be worthless because there is no way I could come up with the money to even get started, so anything you can tell me about the up front investment requirements, recurring costs, and how much of my time would really be required will help me decide if I am interested in buying your book. Based on what you have posted on your website, you seem like an honest guy that is being straight, but I can't afford to be scammed again."*

I would like to post my entire response here and include the analysis spreadsheet that I created for this potential customer, but I would have to make it so small that you couldn't read it, so I will just give you a summary here and let you work with the spreadsheet I have included with the book to draw your own conclusions.

For an online bookseller that starts with an initial inventory of 300 books and a moderate growth expectation to 3,000 books at the end of their first year, it would be reasonable to expect a profit of over $15,000 in that first year, with a paid for inventory of 3,000 books to close out the year. It would also be reasonable to expect your monthly profits to have climbed such that your 12th month of profit is over $2,800.

If you continue to grow your business to a level where you have 7,000 books at the end of three years, you should experience a cumulative profit on the order of $97,000, and your monthly profits should be around $5,000 by the end of your third year. Remember too that at any given point in this analysis, the profits have already accounted for the expense of all the books in your inventory, so at the end of the third year if you have made $97,000, and you have 7,000 books, these books are already paid for and their expense has already been deducted from your gross profits.

I didn't want to hype the scenario, and I used values that are in line with my own experiences as well as those made available by other online booksellers, but I felt it best to provide you with a spreadsheet that you could manipulate with your own values to see for yourself.

---

*"Are there days of the week or times of the year that you find online book sales are better?"*

Yes, but I cannot explain parts of the answer.

For some reason – that I cannot explain, Tuesdays seem to be the best book-selling day of the week. It doesn't seem to have anything to do with when I list new books, although for a few days after I put up new listings I always have a surge in sales. Tuesdays just seem to be the best day of the week for me.

With respect to times of the year that are better than others, I do have an explanation. Book sales are always better just before a new session starts in the universities. College students buy a lot of their texts and required reading materials online. I also have many more sales in the middle of springtime. The springtime surge is probably owing to the fact that I always add to my inventory substantially during this period with books that have been donated to my local library or sold to the local chain bookstore that puts many of them out on the clearance shelves. People tend to do their spring-cleaning and make more donations during this time and I do what I can to supplement my inventory with their donations.

---

*My name is "XXXXXX" and I must say your book seems fascinating and alluring. Your website is well done.*

*The question in my mind is, why publish a book (that as an author you hope will sell well in the marketplace) that will create much competition for you? If I am not mistaken you are still selling books online. It seems that you are sharing trade secrets about the industry to help others succeed. If your book sells well and the information is applied, won't that saturate the market of online book selling?*

*Isn't this a conflict of interests? Or do you think the industry is heading in that direction anyway?*

*Still you have piqued my interest and I am tempted to buy.*

*Thank for your candid response and enlightenment.*

First I would like to thank you for your compliments and taking the time to email me. I have to admit, I had some help setting up my website from my oldest son. The original website I set up was very awkward and time consuming. Nick showed me a few things with Microsoft Front Page, and I have steadily built it up from there.

You are correct about all the statements you made. I am still selling books online and my book would certainly seem to be in contradiction to my own best interest, but the statistician in me tells me the contradiction is not of great concern for many reasons including:

1)      My participation in online bookselling only requires that I shop for inventory within a couple miles of my home and there are already a half dozen other online booksellers that frequent the same places I do, and am still able to maintain a steady inventory.

2)      Even though I might be adding online booksellers to the industry and creating more competition, it is not bad for me if I can teach them to

conduct their business professionally because their buyers will have better online experiences and continue to buy online. If I do not teach new online booksellers the trade and they get into it blindly, they may give buyers a bad experience and the buyers may resort to only buying from brick and mortar stores.

3)    Despite the increasing number of online booksellers in my own area, there does not seem to be any problem finding adequate inventory and this has been the case in my youngest son's area 2,000 miles from mine.

4)    There is also the probability of the numbers to consider. Even if I sell 10,000 of my books (which would be nice) only a small fraction of the buyers will really pursue getting into the business in a scale that would be of significant competition to me or other online booksellers.

Some of this is analogous to the creation of the online marketplace itself in that the big chain book stores, publishers, and even the authors thought Amazon was going to bring down the entire industry by making books so readily available and cheap through the Internet. It doesn't seem to have hurt the industry as a whole, but the industry has had to adapt and be more efficient. The huge publishing houses have had to give up some of their greed based enormous profits and become more efficient, but they are still doing quite well. They have even adopted print on demand technology and some are even selling online directly.

---

# Appendix G
## Spreadsheet Instructions

The accompanying CD has four spreadsheet tools on it, and each is intended for different aspects of the online bookselling business. I will go into the details of each later, but in brief, the spreadsheets are:

1) Break-Even Analysis

This spreadsheet is intended to help you determine the profit/expense break-even point for your own online bookselling business. It is difficult to know the point at which you are profitable if you do not do this analysis.

2) Business Projection

The intent of this spreadsheet is to allow you to input numbers and see what you might expect for income levels for different levels of inventory while realizing different levels of new listing sales and older inventory sales.

3) Running the Numbers

I personally felt it would be doing any prospective online bookseller a disservice to not provide a spreadsheet like this. With this spreadsheet, you can forecast your own inventory/business growth and input your own numbers for such things as average book selling price, and the rate at which you think you can grow your inventory. It does not suffice for me to tell you that such and such can be done and leave it to you to believe me; you need the capability to run the numbers yourself.

4) Bookkeeping for Booksellers

This is the spreadsheet that has held up the release of my book in paperback. I really wanted to provide both the experienced bookseller and the beginner with a spreadsheet that would allow all of your bookkeeping and records to be kept in one place and provide you with tools to prepare your Schedule C as well as your local, and state business taxes. With this tool you will be able to VISUALLY see how your business is doing. It has monthly, quarterly, and annual summaries of almost everything you need for your Schedule C[18], it has 55 graphs to help you visually see how your business is

---

[18] The spreadsheet accounts for all of the income and expenses associated with a typical online bookselling business. Atypical expenses will still need to be accounted for as they arise.

performing, and I felt it was complete enough that I have been using it myself for my own online bookselling business.

With an overview of each of the spreadsheets, I will detail them individually in the remainder of this appendix.

## Break-Even Analysis

This is the simplest of the four spreadsheets and requires minimal inputs on your part. In this spreadsheet, you will enter values in the light grey fields as described, and will be given your calculated break-even point in the light purple field at the bottom of the spreadsheet. I have included a column of example values for you to see the types of input expected. Don't worry, you cannot damage the spreadsheet, I have locked the cells you are not supposed to change so that you could input the numbers you feel are appropriate. If you do manage to corrupt the spreadsheet, you can always read it again from the CD.

## Business Projection

With this spreadsheet I have attempted to demonstrate three levels of online bookselling with my examples and have provided a column for you to input numbers that represent the level you wish to achieve. You can input your own expenses, inventory level, the percent of new listings you anticipate selling, the percentage of older listings you anticipate selling, etc., and the fields in light blue are the ones that should be of interest to you. Again, the fields you should make entries in are in light grey, and all other fields are locked to prevent you from corrupting cells you should not change. This spreadsheet is self-explanatory and allows you to get a feel for the level of online bookselling you personally feel is appropriate for you.

## Running The Numbers

There are several books available about online bookselling and some of the authors paint a very green horizon. Personally, I think online bookselling is great, but I want you to be able to run your own numbers and see for yourself if it is for you, that is the intent of this spreadsheet.

There really isn't much instruction I can give with respect to this spreadsheet, just input your own numbers in the light grey fields and see what you come up with for your own scenario.

## Bookkeeping[19]

I am personally very happy with this spreadsheet. It allows me to keep all of my online bookselling sales and expense records in one place. There are 19 sheets to this spreadsheet, some of which you may choose not to use, but I wanted to include them all to be complete.

The sales page of the spreadsheet allows for 12,000 individual book sale entries, and each of the expense sheets allows for 1,000 respective expense entries. Anything bigger than this would not really be very efficient on a spreadsheet and would require database software.

You can access the different sheets from the tabs at the bottom of the page, they are:

1) Sales – this is where you will enter your individual book sales on a daily basis.
2) Postage Paid – while postage paid is an "Other Expense" as far as your Schedule C is concerned, I wanted to provide you with graphs that show the postage payments you receive against the postage you pay so that you can keep on top of it. Don't worry; the postage paid is accounted for as an "Other Expense" in the summaries so that you will have the appropriate numbers for your taxes.
3) Cost of Goods Sold – this is where you will enter new inventory purchase expenses as well as the number of books purchased with each entry. The reason for entering the number of books purchased with each entry is so that you can refer to the graphs and see whether or not your inventory is growing or shrinking.
4) Commissions & Fees – This is where you will enter your marketplace monthly subscription fees as well as the commissions they charge for books sold.
5) Car & Truck Expenses – this is the sheet on which you can enter odometer readings for the miles you drive your car in conducting your online bookselling business. You can also enter the mileage allowance as allowed by the IRS for the business use of your vehicle.
6) Advertising – if you have advertising expenses for you business, you can enter them on this page of the spreadsheet.
7) Supplies – this is where you will enter expenses such as self-sealing bubble envelopes, packing tape, cleaning materials, etc., used in conducting your online bookselling business.
8) Travel, Meals, & Entertainment – if you travel some distance from your home to buy new inventory, you might wish to take a deduction for the expenses incurred to do this travel. You should refer to the IRS guidelines for travel, meals, & entertainment expenses associated with your business,

---

[19] While I have spent an enormous amount of time checking the accuracy of this spreadsheet, I am not a tax consultant, bookkeeper, or lawyer. I want to make it clear that use of this spreadsheet and reliance on the results is at your own risk. By using this spreadsheet to keep your business records, you are accepting the responsibility for the data entered and the results produced by the spreadsheet, you will not hold me responsible in any way.

but I have included a column for you to enter the deductible percentage of the expense.

9) Taxes & Licenses – you will be paying retail sales tax for the book sales to customers in your own state, and the amount you pay is deductible from your federal taxes. You can also deduct the cost of your business license.

10) Returns – when a customer returns a book, for whatever reason, and you refund them the purchase price as well as shipping, you didn't realize a profit on the original sale and you need to account for the expense of the refund, this is where you will do that.

11) Utilities – if you have utility expenses that are incurred as a result of your online bookselling business, you will enter them here. Some of them that you might want to consider are your cell phone bill and your Internet service provider charge.

12) Other Expenses – if you have other expenses associated with your online bookselling business that do not fit into the other categories, you will enter them here, but do not enter your postage costs again as I have combined postage costs in this category in the summaries.

13) Summary by Month – there is nothing for you to enter on this sheet or any of the following sheets; all of the remaining pages are intended to show you just how your business is performing. This particular sheet will show you on a monthly basis how your sales and expenses stack up.

14) Summary by Quarter – this sheet will show you how sales and expenses look on a quarterly basis.

15) Annual Summary – at the end of the year you can see how you did with respect to sales and expenses, but you do not have to wait until then to look. This sheet like all of the other summary sheets is updated every time you make a sales or expense entry.

16) Monthly Sales Graphs – all the summary tables will tell you the story, but it is the graphs that really show you. On this sheet, you can see:
   a. Gross Sales ($) by month
   b. Books Sold (#) by month
   c. Average Book Selling Price ($) by month
   d. Commissions & Fees ($) by month
   e. Advertising Costs ($) by month
   f. Mileage Costs ($) by month
   g. Supply Costs ($) by month
   h. Travel, Meals, & Entertainment Costs ($) by month
   i. Retail Sales Tax Paid for In-State Sales ($) by month
   j. Returns ($) by month
   k. Inventory Purchases ($) by month
   l. Utilities ($) by month
   m. Other Expenses ($) by month
   n. Gross Profits ($) & Total Expenses ($) by month

17) Quarterly Sales Graphs – like the monthly sales graphs, this is a visual display of the information you have entered on a quarterly basis showing:
   a. Gross Sales ($) by quarter
   b. Books Sold (#) by quarter
   c. Average Book Selling Price ($) by quarter
   d. Commissions & Fees ($) by quarter
   e. Advertising Costs ($) by quarter
   f. Mileage Costs ($) by quarter

   g.   Supply Costs ($) by quarter
   h.   Travel, Meals, & Entertainment Costs ($) by quarter
   i.   Retail Sales Tax Paid for In-State Sales ($) by quarter
   j.   Returns ($) by quarter
   k.   Inventory Purchases ($) by quarter
   l.   Utilities ($) by quarter
   m.   Other Expenses ($) by quarter
   n.   Gross Profits ($) & Total Expenses ($) by quarter

18) Pie Charts – the purpose of the pie charts is to show you the percentages of the pie that make up your total expenses in a graphical form as well as your net profits for each of the twelve months, and the number of books sold each of the twelve months and the four quarters making up the year.

19) Misc. Stats – there were a few things I wanted to provide you with, specifically charts that did not seem to fit appropriately on the other chart pages, so I have included them here. They include:

   a.   Histogram of Shipping Methods – I personally find this information useful because it tells me the relative percentages of books that ship by Media Mail ®, First Class Mail, Priority Mail, international standard deliveries, and international expedited deliveries.

   b.   Histogram of Book Selling Prices – this graph will show you the relative number of books that sold within discrete price ranges so that you can see where most of your sales occur.

   c.   Books Sold & New Inventory Added by Month – if you want to see whether or not your inventory is growing or shrinking, you can look at this graph and tell immediately.

   d.   Inventory Replacement Growth *** Increase by Month – this is a little different way of showing the data in the previous chart, but the results are presented in percentages of growth/shrinkage of inventory.

   e.   Postage Received & Postage Paid by Month – if you want to see whether you are holding your own with respect to shipping costs, you can look at this graph and see if the postage you are being paid is covering what you are paying the post office to ship your books.

Now, with a brief description of each page of the bookkeeping spreadsheet, I would like to address each of the pages individually and explain how to use them and what should be entered on each of them. For the most part, this is very easy to see from the individual sheets, but it warrants some discussion.

## Sales

As the title implies, this is where you will enter your sales on a daily basis, but there are a couple other things to make clear for each of the fields of data entry.

First, all entries you make should only be done in the light grey fields. The entries consist of:

1) Enter the year. This may not seem important, but at the end of the year, you can save this spreadsheet as your records for this particular year and open the

empty spreadsheet from the CD and begin a new year with an empty spreadsheet.

2) Enter your state's retail sales tax rate. You enter 6.5% as 6.5; the field knows the number is a percentage and entering 6.5% as .065 will result in a tax rate of .065%.

3) You need to tell the spreadsheet whether or not your state charges retail sales tax on shipping charges. If your state does charge sales tax on shipping charges, enter "Y" without the quotes, and if not, enter "N" without the quotes. This entry will be used in logic statements within the spreadsheet to determine the amount of retail sales tax you must pay your state for sales to customers in your state.

4) When you are ready to record your sales, enter the month and day of the sale as a number only, e.g., for a sale on May 10 enter a "5" for May in the month column and a "10" for the tenth in the day column. Both should be entered without the quotes.

5) In the SKU / ID column, enter the unique number or identifier for the book that sold. This should be the same as the identifier you used to list the book on the online marketplace.

6) In the Selling Price column, enter the amount that the customer paid for the book, not what you really got for it. The commission will be accounted for elsewhere. You do not need the "$" symbol, the field knows the entry is dollars.

7) In the Shipping Charge field, enter the shipping fee that was paid by the customer, not your shipping reimbursement. Again, the fee charged by the marketplace is accounted for elsewhere and no "$" symbol is required.

8) The Gross Received column is a calculated field; you should not enter anything here.

9) In the In State Sale (Y/N) column, enter a "Y" without quotes if the customer is located in your state. It really isn't necessary to enter an "N" if the sale is an out of state sale, the spreadsheet will default to "N" in the logic calculation if you do not enter an "N."

10) In the Shipping Method column, enter an "M" for a Media Mail ® order, an "F" for a book being shipped by First Class mail, a "P" for a Priority Mail delivery, An "I" for an international deliver via Surface (Economy) Letter Post, or an "X" for a Global Priority expedited international delivery. If you ship by other methods, you will have to categorize these shipments in the above groups.

This is all of the entries for you to make on the Sales page of the spreadsheet. You should enter each book sold separately if you want to see the proper representation in the summaries and graphs.

## Postage Paid

This page is very straightforward. Each day you go to the post office and pay to ship your orders, enter the receipt information on this sheet of the spreadsheet. Do not enter each book separately; just use the total from your post office receipt. Use the same format for the month and date entry as on the Sales page of the spreadsheet.

## Cost of Goods Sold

Because the nature of your business is buying and selling books, the only expense you should be entering here is the cost of new inventory that you have purchased for your business, i.e., there are no costs associated with making your products. Thus, there are a limited number of entries for you to become familiar with here.

First, you need to enter your inventory cost at the beginning of the year (or when you begin your business if you are just starting). This is your actual cost for the books in your inventory either at the beginning of the year, or when you start your business. Just enter the dollar amount without the "$" symbol. This value should be the same as the inventory value at the end of the previous year.

Then enter the value of your inventory at the end of the year. Since you do not know this yet, enter the same value as your beginning of year inventory value entered in the previous step. At the end of the year, you will need to correct this value based on the remaining books in your inventory. Because it is a nightmare to keep track of each and every book's cost, it will probably suffice to use an average book value method, i.e., unless you are buying some very expensive books, you can probably say that every hardback costs $X and every paperback costs $Y and establish your inventory values at the beginning of the year and the end of the year in this manner. Personally, I always know how many books I have in my inventory and I use one value for all of them, but I know this is an almost constant value based on thousands of books bought, and this is the number I use at the end of the year to calculate my end of year inventory value. Be consistent.

The rest of the entries on this page are similar to entries on other pages, but there is one other new entry to be made, the Quantity Purchased entry. The reason for making this entry is to keep track of the number of books bought and sold so that you can see if your inventory is growing or shrinking. When you go out and buy books at various places, keep track of how many were purchased from each place and enter this quantity when you are entering other receipt information here.

## Commissions & Fees

This is where you will enter all the various marketplace commissions and fees. Don't enter them individually; enter the values given in your monthly statements from the marketplaces. They will tell you how much they have charged you (a total) for both commissions and fees. For example, if Amazon charged you $39.99 for your marketplace-listing fee and 257.38 in selling commissions, enter the total of $297.37 in one entry and describe it as your Amazon listing fee and commissions for the date of the statement.

## Car & Truck Expenses (Mileage)

This is where you will keep track of the miles you drove your car or truck in conducting your online bookselling business. You will also need to enter the current rate as allowed by the IRS for vehicle mileage. This is one expense that many online booksellers do not take a deduction for because they forget to write down their odometer readings for the short trips they make. These miles add up fast and you should get a notebook to keep in your car/truck to keep track of them. You can bring the notebook in your house once a month and enter the information in your spreadsheet, or whenever it is convenient for you.

## Advertising

You are not likely to have very many advertising expenses, but in the event that you do have some, this is where you will enter them. Some of the ones that I record include the cost of my website, the cost of business cards and printed bookmarks, and the cost of advertising my book.

## Supplies

Entries on this sheet are done in the same manner as other sheets, and the types of expenses include, self-sealing bubble pack envelopes, packing tape, Scotch® tape, staples, stretch and shrink wrap, pens, pencils, etc.

## Travel, Meals, & Entertainment

If like me, you travel to locations away from your home that require you to stay in a hotel, eat out, etc., to find new inventory for your business, you are entitled to deduct a part of your incurred expenses. Remember to keep receipts to substantiate your claims, and keep a record of the percentage of the trip that is exclusively business related. Since I combine these trips with personal leisure, and you may too, it is important to keep records of how much of the trip was for pleasure and how much was for business. Even if the entire trip is exclusively for business, you cannot deduct all of the expenses and should refer to the IRS guidelines to determine what percent can be deducted. That is why I included a field for Business Percentage. This is intended to be the percentage of cost deduction that the IRS allows. Thus, if you have expenses for a trip that total $379.85 and the trip was 50% leisure and 50% business, enter half of the $379.85 as the expense, or $189.92. Then, in the Business Percentage, enter the IRS allowable deduction percentage of say 50% (refer to IRS guidelines for the actual allowable percentage) and the spreadsheet will calculate an allowable expense of $94.96.

## Taxes & Licenses

Enter the actual tax and/or license fees you incur here, but do not include retail sales tax paid for books sold to customers in you state, this has already been accounted for elsewhere and you do not want to duplicate it here.

## Returns

When a customer returns a book and you give them a refund, record the information here so that you take the appropriate deduction from your sales proceeds. You do not want to pay federal income tax on the proceeds of a book sold if it is returned.

## Utilities

Enter the cost of utilities associated with your business here, including the portion of your cell phone bill that you can attribute to your business and the cost of your Internet Service Provider. Include only the percentage of these utilities that can be attributed to the business. If you use your computer to surf the Internet for personal reasons, you cannot deduct 100% of the cost for your Internet Service Provider as a business expense. Similarly, if you do not use your cell phone exclusively for your business, you cannot deduct 100% of the monthly bill for business use.

## Other Expenses

This is where you can enter any other expenses associated with your business including tax preparation software, or any other legitimate deduction that has not been accounted for and does not have an appropriate field on your Schedule C.

## Summary by Month

While there are no entries for you to make on this sheet, there is at least one thing you should be aware of, the retail sales tax paid on in-state sales should be added to the taxes & licenses field for tax form purposes. I intentionally left them separate here so you could easily see how much retail sales tax you are obligated to pay your state for books sold to customers in your state.

There is a summary for each of the twelve months of the year on this sheet and you can use the scroll bar on the side of the page to see the months that do not appear.

## Summary by Quarter

The quarters are defined as:

Quarter 1 – January, February, & March
Quarter 2 – April, May, & June
Quarter 3 – July August, & September
Quarter 4 – October, November, & December

Like the summary by month page, you should combine the retail sales tax paid on in-state sales and the taxes & licenses fields for tax form purposes. Again, I left them separate because some states require retail sales tax to be paid quarterly and I felt it was more convenient for you to see it separately.

## Annual Summary

Unless you have expenses that are not included in this spreadsheet, e.g., contract labor costs, depletion, depreciation and section 179 expense deductions, employee benefits, etc., this page will provide you with the information you need for filling out your Schedule C with your IRS tax return. Again, you will need to combine retail sales tax paid on in-state sales and the taxes & licenses field for tax form purposes. It also provides you with a sales, expenses, and profit summary.

## Monthly Sales Graphs

Most of the graphs on age are very easy to understand and do not require any explanation, but I do want to tell you a little about the last graph, the Gross Profit & Total Expenses graph. The purpose of this graph is to show you pictorially the magnitude of your profits and expenses on a monthly basis. If the two columns for any given month are the same height, your profits and expenses are not canceling each other, it simply means that your profit is equal in magnitude to your expenses, i.e., if both are $1,000.00, then it says that it cost you $1,000.00 to make $1,000.00 profit and the risk to reward ratio would be 1.0 because you risked $1,000.00 to make $1,000.00 profit. Similarly, if your profit was $2,500.00 and your expenses were $500.00 then your risk to reward ration would be 0.20 (risk = $500, divided by reward = $2,500.00, results in $500/$2,500 or 0.2).

The bigger the profit bar is in comparison to the expense bar, the better your business is doing.

## Quarterly Sales Graphs

The graphs on this sheet are the same as those on the monthly sales graphs page with the data from the months combines as described below:

Quarter 1 – January, February, & March
Quarter 2 – April, May, & June
Quarter 3 – July August, & September
Quarter 4 – October, November, & December

The only graph here that really needs any discussion is the Gross Profit & Total Expenses graph, which is explained above in the monthly sales graphs discussion, but represented here by quarters.

## Pie Charts

This is a collection of graphs that show you pictorially how all things in the individual graphs add up to make a complete pie. For example, when you look at your January expense pie chart (the first one on the sheet) you will see a pie with slices of varying sizes. The slices are proportional to the individual expenses that make up the whole pie. I tried to put the data labels on the slices, but there was just too much text being displayed and it could not be read. I opted to put the color-coded legend on each chart and if you want to see the numbers being represented by the various slices, just put your cursor on the slice you want to know about and the description, and the numbers, and the percentage of the entire pie will appear.

You can browse through the various pie charts on this sheet and learn a lot about the expenses your own online bookselling business is realizing.

## Misc. Stats.

These are the charts I refer to the most because I want to know how many books are shipping by what methods, the relative number of books selling for different price ranges, if I am buying and adding as many books as I am selling, what percent growth or shrinkage my inventory is experiencing, and whether the postage I am receiving is at least as great as the postage I am paying. The graphs are easy to understand and I am sure you will find them useful for your online bookselling business.

I sincerely hope you find this spreadsheet as useful as I do; I certainly spent a lot of time to make it and would not have invested the time if I did not see a benefit for the online bookseller. Your comments, suggestions, and criticism (if constructive) would be appreciated.

# Index

## A

## B

# S

# T

# U

# V

# W

# X Y Z

**No Entries**

# Notes

# Notes

# Notes